Introduction to A

by Gilad James, I

Copyright

I. Introduction

1. Definition of Afghanistan

Introduction

Afghanistan, officially known as the Islamic Republic of Afghanistan, is a landlocked country located in South Asia and Central Asia. The country is bordered by Pakistan to the east and south, Iran to the west, Turkmenistan, Uzbekistan, and Tajikistan to the north, and China to the northeast. The country's capital city is Kabul, which is also its largest city. Afghanistan has a rich history and culture and has been influenced by various empires, including the Persian Empire, the Greco-Bactrian Kingdom, the Mongol Empire, the Timurid Empire, and the Mughal Empire.

Definition of Afghanistan

Afghanistan is a country rich in history and culture, and it is known for its rugged and mountainous terrain. It is a country that has been ravaged by war and conflict for many years. The country is known for its strategic location, which has made it an important center for trade and commerce. Afghanistan has a diverse population with a variety of ethnic groups, languages, and religions. The official languages of Afghanistan are Dari and Pashto, and the major religions practiced in the country are Islam and Hinduism.

Geography and Climate

Afghanistan is a landlocked country located in South Asia and Central Asia. The country is situated between Pakistan to the east and south, Iran to the west, Turkmenistan, Uzbekistan, and Tajikistan to the north, and China to the northeast. The country's total area is 652,230 square kilometers, and it is the 40th largest country in the world. The country is mostly mountainous, with the Hindu Kush range running along the northeast and the Afghanistan-Pakistan border. The country's highest peak is Nowshak, which is 7,485 meters high.

Afghanistan has a dry climate, with hot summers and cold winters. The country has four seasons, including spring, summer, fall, and winter. The summers are hot and dry, with temperatures reaching up to 45 degrees Celsius in some areas. The winters are cold and snowy, with temperatures dropping below zero degrees Celsius. The country receives very little rainfall throughout the year, with most of the precipitation occurring in the spring and winter months.

History of Afghanistan

Afghanistan has a rich history that dates back to ancient times. The land now known as Afghanistan has been inhabited by various tribes and civilizations over the years, including the Achaemenid Empire, the Alexander the Great, the Mauryan Empire, the Greco-Bactrian Kingdom, the Kushan Empire, and the Islamic Caliphate. In the 19th century, Afghanistan was invaded by the British Empire, which resulted in the country becoming a buffer state between British India and the Russian Empire.

In 1919, Afghanistan gained independence from British rule and became a constitutional monarchy. However, the country was beset by political instability and coups over the years that followed. In 1978, the Saur Revolution took place, and the Communist Party took power in Afghanistan. The revolution was met with resistance, and a civil war broke out in the country. In 1989, the Soviet Union, which had invaded Afghanistan in 1979 to prop up the communist government, withdrew its troops, leaving behind a country in shambles.

The Taliban, an extremist Islamic group, rose to power in Afghanistan in the 1990s and imposed a strict version of Sharia law on the country. In 2001, after the September 11 attacks in the United States, the US and its allies invaded Afghanistan and overthrew the Taliban government. Since then, Afghanistan has been under a Western-backed government, but the country continues to be marred by violence and conflict.

Economy of Afghanistan

Afghanistan has a largely agricultural economy, and the country's main exports are opium, fruits, and nuts. The country is also rich in natural resources, including iron ore, copper, lithium, and rare earth elements. However, most of these resources are largely untapped due to years of war and conflict. The country is one of the poorest in the world, with a per capita GDP of $502 in 2020.

The war and conflict in Afghanistan have had a devastating impact on the country's economy. The country's infrastructure has been destroyed, and many of its people have been displaced. The opium trade has also fueled corruption and violence in the country. The US and its allies have poured millions of dollars into the country's economy to try to rebuild it, but progress has been slow, and the country remains heavily dependent on foreign aid.

Culture of Afghanistan

Afghanistan has a rich and diverse culture that has been shaped by its history and geography. The country's culture is a blend of various ethnicities, languages, and religions. The country's official languages are Dari and Pashto, and the major religions practiced in the country are Islam and Hinduism.

Afghanistan is known for its arts and crafts, including pottery, weaving, embroidery, and woodworking. The country is also known for its traditional music and dance, which are often performed at weddings and other celebrations. The cuisine of Afghanistan is also an important part of its culture, with dishes such as kabuli pulao, mantu, and ashak being popular.

Conclusion

Afghanistan is a country with a rich history and culture, but it has been marred by years of war and conflict. The country's strategic location has made it an important center for trade and commerce, but its position has also made it a target for invasion and occupation. The country's economy is largely agricultural, and it is one of the poorest in the world. The country continues to be plagued by violence and political instability, but its people remain resilient and proud of their heritage.

2. Historical background of Afghanistan

Introduction

Afghanistan has a long and turbulent history, which has been shaped by both domestic and foreign powers. The country has been strategically located at the crossroads of major trade routes and has been coveted by various empires throughout history. In this paper, we will explore the historical background of Afghanistan in relation to its introduction. We will examine the major empires that have controlled and influenced the region, including the Persian Empire, Alexander the Great's conquest, the rule of the Mughal Empire, the British Raj, and the Soviet Union. We will also discuss the impact of religion, specifically Islam, on Afghanistan's history and culture.

The Persian Empire

The Persians were the first major power to control Afghanistan. The Achaemenid Persian Empire, which began in 550 BCE, extended its control from the eastern Mediterranean to the Indus River in present-day Pakistan. Afghanistan served as a vital buffer between the Persian Empire and the various nomadic tribes that occupied Central Asia. During the reign of Darius I, the Persian Empire established the satrapy of Gandhara, which included modern-day Afghanistan, Pakistan, and part of India. This region became an important center of trade and culture, with many of the famous Buddhist relics, such as the Bamiyan Buddha statues, being created during this period.

Alexander the Great's Conquest

Alexander the Great's invasion of Afghanistan in 330 BCE marked a significant moment in Afghanistan's history. Despite fierce resistance from local tribes, Alexander conquered the region within three years. He founded the city of Alexandria on the Oxus, which became an important center of trade and culture. Alexander's legacy in Afghanistan was the spread of Greek culture and the introduction of Hellenistic art, which influenced the development of Buddhist art in the region.

The Mughal Empire

In the 16th century, the Mughal Empire extended its control to Afghanistan. Babur, the founder of the Mughal Empire, was born in present-day Uzbekistan and migrated to India. In 1526, he defeated the Sultan of Delhi and established the Mughal Empire. The Mughals controlled Afghanistan for a brief period in the 16th century before being ousted by the Safavid dynasty of Persia. The Mughals returned to Afghanistan in the 17th century, and their rule was marked by the construction of numerous architectural marvels, such as the mausoleum of Emperor Jahangir in Kabul.

The British Raj

The British Raj, which spanned from 1858 to 1947, marked a significant shift in Afghanistan's history. Afghanistan became a buffer state between British India and the Russian Empire, which set the stage for the Great Game, a geopolitical struggle between Russia and Britain for control of Central Asia. The British established diplomatic relations with Afghanistan in 1809 and later attempted to annex the country following the Second Anglo-Afghan War in 1878. British control over Afghanistan was tenuous, and they faced fierce resistance from Afghan tribes, who resented foreign interference. In 1919, Afghanistan gained independence from British control, although British influence remained significant until the mid-20th century.

Soviet Intervention

The Soviet Union's intervention in Afghanistan in 1979 marks a particularly turbulent moment in Afghanistan's history. The Soviet Union had been a key ally of Afghanistan since the 1950s, and in 1978, a Communist Party-led coup overthrew the government. The Soviet Union invaded Afghanistan in response to the growing Islamist rebellion, which was seen as a threat to Soviet interests in Central Asia. The Soviet Union withdrew its troops from Afghanistan in 1989, after a decade of bloody conflict that led to the deaths of thousands of people. The withdrawal of Soviet troops marked the end of the Cold War and the start of a period of instability that continues to this day.

Religion in Afghanistan

GILAD JAMES

Islam has been a key factor in Afghanistan's history and culture. Afghanistan has been a predominantly Muslim country since the 7th century, when Arab conquerors introduced Islam to the region. Islam has played a significant role in shaping Afghanistan's politics, culture, and society. The Taliban regime, which ruled Afghanistan from 1996 to 2001, was a particularly extremist interpretation of Islam that imposed strict laws and norms on women and minorities. The Taliban's regime was marked by brutal repression of dissent and human rights abuses.

Conclusion

Afghanistan's history has been shaped by both domestic and foreign powers. The country has been strategically located at the crossroads of major trade routes, which has made it an attractive target for empires throughout history. Afghanistan's history has also been shaped by religion, specifically Islam, which has played a significant role in shaping its politics, culture, and society. The impact of foreign powers on Afghanistan's history has been particularly significant, and the country's fragile political landscape continues to be shaped by outside forces. Despite these challenges, Afghanistan has a rich cultural heritage that reflects its complex history and diverse society.

3. Importance of studying Afghanistan

Introduction

Afghanistan is a landlocked country located in Central and South Asia. It is a developing nation with a significant history that has shaped its current political, social, and economic status. The country has been the subject of brutal political turmoil for years, and it has witnessed prolonged episodes of foreign invasions, occupation, and regional instability that have impacted its social and economic state. Despite the challenging conditions, Afghanistan has been a valuable place of study for scholars and researchers for its rich cultural heritage, regional significance, and strategic position as a gateway between Central and South Asia. This paper seeks to highlight the importance of studying Afghanistan in contemporary times and the benefits it presents to the academic community.

Historical significance

The study of Afghanistan holds immense importance from an academic standpoint, especially concerning its historical significance. The country is a melting pot of numerous cultures and civilizations that have contributed to shaping its identity over time. Afghanistan is a historical site for many crucial events and movements that impacted the region and the world at large. For example, the conquest of Alexander the Great, which played an essential role in the spread of Hellenistic culture in Central Asia, began with the invasion of Afghanistan. Similarly, it was a significant center of the Kushan empire,

and it played a crucial role in the spread of Buddhism in the region.
These historical events and movements have had a profound impact
on Afghanistan's culture, religion, and political thought, making them
crucial areas of study for researchers and scholars.

Strategic significance

Geopolitically, Afghanistan holds immense importance in the region
due to its strategic location as a connecting link between Central and
South Asia. The country borders Pakistan, Iran, Turkmenistan,
Uzbekistan, and Tajikistan, making it an essential land bridge between
the two regions. Afghanistan has been a major crossroads for various
trade routes and has been a point of commercial and cultural exchange
since ancient times. The country's strategic significance has drawn the
attention of powerful states such as the United States, China, Russia,
and neighboring countries such as Iran and Pakistan, who have
significant interests in the region. From an academic standpoint,
Afghanistan's strategic position provides researchers with an avenue to
explore the interactions between various states and how they shape the
country's political and economic conditions.

Socioeconomic significance

Afghanistan's socioeconomic status presents a vast area of study as it is
considered one of the poorest and least developed countries globally.
The protracted conflicts and political instability the country has
witnessed over the years have significantly affected its economic
development. The country mostly relies on agriculture and natural

resources, such as minerals and petroleum, as its primary sources of income. Afghan citizens' precarious socioeconomic conditions due to a weak education system, poverty, and limited access to healthcare services are essential areas of study for understanding the country's current state. Scholars and researchers who examine Afghanistan's economy and social issues can provide insights into the challenges the country faces, propose solutions, and offer innovative strategies that could potentially lead to sustainable development.

Political importance

Afghanistan has been unstable politically, with several internal conflicts and the intervention of outside powers over the past few decades. The Soviet invasion in 1979 that led to a decade-long war between Soviet-backed Afghan government and Mujahedin groups became a gateway for regional and global powers to be involved in internal Afghan conflict. The Taliban regime's takeover in 1996 followed by the US-led invasion of Afghanistan in 2001 has left the country with a weak democratic government that still continues to face security threats and political turmoil. The ongoing conflict and instability have contributed to the resurgence of the Taliban, and the situation has become a source of regional and international concern. A study of the country's political history, the current political landscape, and the complex web of actors involved in the conflict provides a unique insight into the political dynamics of the region. Understanding the political intricacies of Afghanistan can be useful in managing regional and global security concerns and shaping regional policies towards the country.

Cultural importance

Afghanistan's cultural heritage is diverse, having been a crossroads of various civilizations and cultures over the centuries. The country boasts an intricate blend of traditional and modern cultural practices and is home to numerous ethnic groups. The country's rich cultural heritage is visible in its music, literature, art, and architecture, among others. Afghanistan's strategic location and cross-cultural interactions with other regions have contributed to this rich heritage. From an academic perspective, studying Afghanistan's vibrant culture provides a glimpse into the country's identity, history, and various influences that have shaped its cultural heritage through centuries.

Security significance

Afghanistan's security implications are of significant concern globally, as the country's instability and ongoing conflict have had spillover effects on neighboring countries and regions. Terrorism, drug trafficking, and the migration of terrorism-laden ideologies have all impacted Afghanistan and the wider region's security. As a result, Afghanistan has become an important theater for regional and international security concerns, and the study of security implications helps researchers to understand the nature of these security threats and how they potentially impact the country's social, enconomic and political development.

Conclusion

Studying Afghanistan is critical for a better understanding of the country's history, culture, socio-economic and political context, security implications, and strategic importance. Afghanistan presents numerous opportunities for researchers and scholars to explore many crucial areas of academics, which has beneficiaries to both the academic institutions and the wider world. The threats and opportunities presented by Afghanistan's landscape make it a fascinating and relevant subject for researchers, particularly in the fields of International Relations, Political Science, Strategic Studies, History, Economics and Sociology.

4. Quiz

to Afghanistan

1. What is the official language of Afghanistan?
   a. Farsi
   b. Pashto
   c. Dari
   d. Arabic

2. What is Afghanistan's currency?
   a. Afghan rupee
   b. Afghan dinar
   c. Afghan afghani
   d. Afghan rial

3. What religion is most commonly practiced in Afghanistan?
   a. Christianity
   b. Buddhism
   c. Hinduism
   d. Islam

4. What is the approximate population of Afghanistan?
   a. 10 million
   b. 25 million
   c. 35 million
   d. 50 million

5. What is Afghanistan's largest city?
   a. Herat
   b. Mazar-i-Sharif
   c. Kabul
   d. Kandahar

6. Which neighboring country shares the longest border with Afghanistan?
   a. India
   b. Pakistan
   c. Iran
   d. China

7. When did the Taliban take control of Afghanistan?
   a. 1992
   b. 1996
   c. 2001
   d. 2005

8. What is Afghanistan's national sport?
   a. Cricket
   b. Soccer
   c. Wrestling
   d. Baseball

9. What is the main export of Afghanistan?

a. Opium
b. Oil
c. Gold
d. Diamonds

10. What major event occurred on September 11, 2001, that had a profound impact on Afghanistan?
   a. The assassination of the Taliban leader
   b. The U.S. invasion of Afghanistan
   c. The signing of a peace agreement with neighboring countries
   d. The construction of a new international airport in Kabul

Answers:
   1. c. Dari
   2. c. Afghan afghani
   3. d. Islam
   4. c. 35 million
   5. c. Kabul
   6. b. Pakistan
   7. b. 1996
   8. c. Wrestling
   9. a. Opium
   10. b. The U.S. invasion of Afghanistan

II. Geography and Climate

1. Location and borders

Introduction to Afghanistan: Location and Borders

Afghanistan is a landlocked country situated in South Asia, bordered by Pakistan to the east and south, Iran to the west, Turkmenistan, Uzbekistan, and Tajikistan to the north, and China to the northeast. Afghanistan's geographical location has shaped its history, politics, culture, and economy in various ways. Therefore, it is imperative to understand Afghanistan's location, borders, and regional dynamics to understand the country's complexities and challenges. This paper discusses Afghanistan's location, borders history, and current political and economic implications.

Location

Afghanistan is located between 29°30' and 38° latitude north of the equator and between 60° and 75° longitude east of the Greenwich Meridian. It shares a 1,338-kilometer (830 miles) border with Pakistan, a 936-kilometer (582 miles) border with Iran, a 144-kilometer (89.5 miles) border with China, a 1,206-kilometer (749 miles) border with Turkmenistan, a 1,206-kilometer (749 miles) border with Uzbekistan, and a 1,510-kilometer (938 miles) border with Tajikistan. Afghanistan's total land area is 652,230 square kilometers (251,827 square miles), making it the 40th largest country in the world, slightly smaller than the U.S. state of Texas.

Afghanistan's geography is characterized by mountain ranges, valleys, steppes, deserts, and river systems. The Hindukush mountain range forms the central and eastern part of the country and separates Afghanistan from Pakistan. The range also hosts several peaks above 7,000 meters (23,000 feet), including Noshaq, the country's highest peak at 7,492 meters (24,580 feet). The Pamir and Karakoram ranges, which extend towards China, form Afghanistan's northeastern border. Other major mountain ranges in Afghanistan include the Safed Koh, Sulaiman, and Koh-i-Baba. The central highlands of the country account for nearly two-thirds of the country's land area, where the average elevation is above 2,000 meters (6,560 feet).

Several rivers flow through Afghanistan, including the Amu Darya, which forms its northern border with Tajikistan, the Oxus River, Helmand River, and Kabul River. The presence of water resources contributes to the country's agriculture and hydropower potential. However, Afghanistan's geography also poses significant challenges to its development, such as limited arable land, water scarcity, and harsh climatic conditions.

Borders History

Afghanistan is situated at the crossroads of ancient trade routes that connected the Middle East, South Asia, and Central Asia. Over the centuries, the country has been invaded, colonized, and ruled by various outside forces, including Alexander the Great, Genghis Khan, the Persians, the British, the Soviets, and the Americans. These invasions and conquests have redrawn Afghanistan's borders and influenced its political, social, and cultural development.

One of the most significant border disputes in Afghanistan's history is the Durand Line, which divides Afghanistan and Pakistan. The line was drawn in 1893 by British colonial officials to demarcate their sphere of influence and control over the Pashtun tribes living on both sides of the border. However, the Durand Line has never been recognized as a formal border by successive Afghan governments, which argue that it was imposed upon them by external powers without their consent. The border has been a source of tension and conflict between Afghanistan and Pakistan, with each accusing the other of harboring rebels, militants, and terrorists.

Another border dispute concerns the Wakhan Corridor, a narrow strip of land that connects Afghanistan to China. The Corridor was created as a buffer zone between the Russian and British Empires in the late 19th century and has remained a remote and sparsely populated area since then. However, the recent Chinese investments in the region for infrastructure development and mining have raised concerns among Afghan officials about Chinese influence and land grabs.

Afghanistan's borders with Iran and Central Asian countries were also drawn by external powers during the 19th and 20th centuries. However, they have been relatively stable and sealed off due to international sanctions and border control measures. The Afghan government has been seeking to improve its relations and economic ties with its neighbors, but the ongoing conflicts, political instability, and insecurity in the country have hampered these efforts.

Current Political and Economic Implications

Afghanistan's location and borders have significant political and economic implications for itself and the region. The country has been prone to foreign intervention, proxy wars, and cross-border terrorism due to its strategic location and porous borders. In recent decades, Afghanistan has become a battleground for global and regional powers seeking to advance their interests and influence through supporting rival factions and militias.

The ongoing conflict in Afghanistan has spilled over into its neighboring countries, exacerbating regional instability and insecurity. The Taliban, a militant group that seeks to establish an Islamic Emirate of Afghanistan, has bases and sanctuaries in Pakistan, which has been accused of providing them with support and shelter. The presence of terrorist groups such as Al-Qaeda, ISIS, and Lashkar-e-Taiba in the region has heightened security concerns for Afghanistan and its neighbors.

Afghanistan's location also affects its economic prospects. The country is landlocked, which means it has limited access to the sea and international markets. The difficult terrain, inadequate infrastructure, and security challenges make it costly and risky to transport goods and services across the borders. The country heavily relies on imports for its basic needs, such as food, fuel, and medicine, which are vulnerable to supply disruptions and price fluctuations.

However, Afghanistan also has significant economic potential, especially in the areas of mining, agriculture, and energy. The country is estimated to have rich reserves of lithium, copper, gold, and other minerals, which could fetch billions of dollars in revenues if properly explored and extracted. Afghanistan also has vast tracts of arable land, favorable climatic conditions, and water resources that could support agriculture and livestock production. The country also has high potential for renewable energy sources, such as solar, wind, and hydroelectric power.

The Afghan government and its international partners have been working to develop the country's infrastructure, legal framework, and human capital to unlock its economic potential. However, progress has been slow and uneven due to the ongoing conflict and corruption. The COVID-19 pandemic has further hampered Afghanistan's economic recovery, with the country facing a sharp decline in revenue, remittances, and aid.

Conclusion

In conclusion, Afghanistan's location and borders have played a significant role in shaping its history, politics, culture, and economy. The country's strategic location at the heart of South Asia has made it a battleground for global and regional powers seeking to advance their interests and influence. The country's borders have been a source of tension and conflict, especially the Durand Line, which divides Afghanistan and Pakistan. Afghanistan's landlocked geography, difficult terrain, and porous borders have posed significant challenges to its economic development. However, the country also has significant economic potential, especially in the areas of mining, agriculture, and energy. The ongoing conflict, political instability, and insecurity have hampered Afghanistan's efforts to unlock its economic potential and improve its relations with its neighbors. Therefore, it is imperative for the Afghan government and its international partners to address these challenges and sustainably develop the country's economy and infrastructure.

2. Topography and land use

Introduction

Afghanistan is a country located in South Asia and Central Asia. It is bordered by China in the east, Pakistan in the south, Iran in the west, Turkmenistan, Uzbekistan, and Tajikistan in the north. Afghanistan is known for its rich history, cultural diversity, and its unique terrain. The topography and land use have played a crucial role in shaping the country's economy and political landscape. In this paper, we will explore the topography and land use in Afghanistan, their relationship, and how they have influenced the country's development.

Topography of Afghanistan

Afghanistan's topography is diverse and rugged, encompassing vast mountain ranges, high plateaus, vast deserts, river valleys, and fertile plains. Its topography makes it one of the most challenging terrains globally, speckled with natural and human-made obstacles. The Hindu Kush mountain range, which runs from central Afghanistan to northern Pakistan, dominates the country's landscape. Other significant mountain ranges include the Pamir mountains, the Safed Koh range, and the Sulaiman Mountains.

The highest peak in Afghanistan is Noshaq, which stands at 7,430meters above sea level, making it the second-highest peak in South Asia. The country's terrain is characterized by sharp, steep mountains, barren valleys, and deep ravines, making it a challenging terrain for infrastructure development. The harsh topography of the country has also played a significant role in shaping the country's political and social landscape, contributing to the formation of isolated communities and entrenched tribalism.

Land use in Afghanistan

Afghanistan's land use is heavily influenced by its topography, as different regions have varying soil types, climates, and a wide variety of ecosystems. Agriculture is a crucial sector of the country's economy and employs over 80% of the population. However, due to the rugged terrain, only 12% of the country's land is suitable for agriculture, with the majority confined to fertile river valleys such as the Helmand and Kabul rivers.

Crops cultivated in Afghanistan include cereals such as wheat, corn, rice, and barley, vegetables such as potatoes, onions, and tomatoes, and fruits such as apples, grapes, and apricots. The country is a significant producer of opium, which is used in the production of heroin. Cash crops such as cotton, tobacco, and marijuana have also grown in different parts of the country.

Mining is also an essential sector of the country's economy. Afghanistan is rich in natural resources such as copper, iron ore, gold, silver, and lapis lazuli. The country also has substantial reserves of natural gas and oil, which have not been fully exploited due to the country's political instability. The extraction of these resources is often difficult due to the country's terrain and the lack of infrastructure.

Livestock grazing is also a significant sector of Afghanistan's economy, with millions of people depending on pastoralism for their daily livelihoods. The difficult terrain of the country has made it suitable for raising sheep, goats, cows, and camels, which can survive on the rugged land. Livestock is a significant source of food, leather, and wool and is sold in local and international markets.

Impact of topography on land use

Due to the challenging terrain of Afghanistan, infrastructure development has been a significant challenge. The rugged topography has meant that roads, bridges, and railroads are expensive to construct and maintain. As such, most of Afghanistan's infrastructure is limited to a few major cities such as Kabul, Herat, and Jalalabad. The harsh topography has also contributed to the country's political instability, with isolated communities and regions contributing to the development of deep-seated tribalism, which has lent itself to violent conflicts over resources.

The mountainous topography has also limited agricultural activities, with only a small percentage of arable land available for farming. Irrigation is a significant challenge due to the rugged terrain, and reliance on rain-fed agriculture has made the livelihoods of millions of Afghans vulnerable to climate change.

The rugged terrain has also contributed to the difficulty of enforcing property rights. Due to the absence of proper mapping and infrastructure, boundary disputes are common in rural areas. As such, disputes over land have been a significant driver of conflict in the country.

Human impact on land use

The rugged topography of Afghanistan has enabled its various ethnic groups and communities to live largely isolated lives. As such, each community has developed its own unique ways of utilizing the land. Historically, nomadic tribes would move from one region to another, depending on the availability of resources such as water, fodder, and grazing lands. However, due to the growing influence of modernization, many nomadic communities have settled in urban areas, leading to challenges such as overcrowding and unemployment.

The high demand for resources such as wood and water has also led to environmental degradation. Deforestation has largely depleted the country's forests, leading to soil erosion, landslides, and floods. Overgrazing has also led to the degradation of pasturelands, contributing to desertification in some regions.

Land use policies

The Afghan government has recognized the importance of sustainable land use and has put in place policies to guide and regulate land use activities. The Afghan Constitution recognizes land as public property and obliges the government to protect and preserve it for the benefit of all citizens. The government has also established the Ministry of Agriculture, Irrigation, and Livestock, which is responsible for promoting sustainable agricultural practices and ensuring food security.

The government has also established policies and programs aimed at addressing environmental degradation. The National Environmental Protection Agency is responsible for implementing environmental policies and regulations aimed at protecting the environment and natural resources.

Conclusion

The topography and land use of Afghanistan have played a significant role in shaping the country's economy, society, and political landscape. The rugged terrain has made infrastructure development a significant challenge, leading to isolation and deep-seated tribalism in some regions. The harsh topography has also made agricultural activities difficult, limiting the country's potential for food security. The country's diverse topography has enabled each community to develop its unique ways of utilizing land, leading to a range of sustainable and unsustainable land use practices. The Afghan government has recognized the importance of sustainable land use and has established policies aimed at addressing environmental degradation and promoting sustainable agricultural practices.

3. Climate and weather patterns

Introduction

Afghanistan is a landlocked country located in South Asia between Iran, Pakistan, Tajikistan, Uzbekistan, and Turkmenistan. Afghanistan has a terrain mountainous, with over fifty percent of its land covered by mountains. The country is known to have diverse climatic zones, which include arid, semi-arid, subtropical, and alpine. The country also experiences varying weather patterns throughout the year. This paper examines climate and weather patterns in Afghanistan and how they affect the country's economy, agriculture, and social life.

Climate patterns in Afghanistan

Afghanistan is known to have a continental climate. The country is dry and arid, with low precipitation levels throughout the year. The non-mountainous areas of Afghanistan have warm summers and cold winters. The average temperature in the summer ranges between 30°C to 35°C while in winter, the temperature can drop as low as -15°C. However, during winter and spring, the country experiences high winds and dust storms that can cause respiratory problems to the population.

The mountainous regions of Afghanistan experience different climate zones based on their elevations. The higher elevations have harsher and colder weather than the lower elevations. At elevations above 3,000 meters, the weather is cold throughout the year, while at elevations between 1,200 to 1,500 meters, the weather is mild with cool summers and cold winters.

The rainfall pattern in Afghanistan varies throughout the country. The southern and western regions of the country are known to be arid with low precipitation levels averaging between 100-200 mm per year. However, the mountainous regions in the east and northeast regions of the country experience higher precipitation levels averaging between 400-700 mm per year. The precipitation levels in Afghanistan are highly variable, with some regions experiencing rainfall shortages and droughts.

Weather patterns in Afghanistan

Afghanistan experiences four distinct seasons throughout the year, which include spring, summer, fall, and winter. During the summer season, the country experiences hot and dry weather, which lasts from June to September. The average temperature during this period ranges between 30°C to 35°C. During the hottest days of the season, the temperature can rise up to 45°C. During this period, the population relies on irrigation methods to sustain the agriculture sector as there is no rainfall to support crop growth.

During the fall season, the weather patterns in Afghanistan begin to change, and the temperatures become cooler. The autumn season lasts from October to November. During this season, the population in

Afghanistan prepare their farms for the winter season, which brings harsh weather conditions.

The winter season lasts from December to February, and it is the coldest time of the year in Afghanistan. During this season, the country experiences snowfall, which is crucial in sustaining agriculture during the next growing season. The average temperature during this period is between -5°C to -10°C, with the highest elevations experiencing temperatures as low as -30°C.

The spring season in Afghanistan lasts from March to May, and it brings warmer weather conditions as the temperatures begin to rise. The temperatures during the spring season range between 20°C to 25°C, and the population begins to prepare their farms for the growing season.

Climate change in Afghanistan

Climate change is a growing concern in Afghanistan, with the country already experiencing its effects. Over the last few decades, Afghanistan has experienced several extreme weather events that have impacted the country's economy and agriculture sector. The increase in temperature and changes in rainfall patterns have led to water scarcity and droughts, which have severely affected the agriculture sector.

The extreme weather events have caused food insecurity in the country, leading to an increase in malnutrition cases. The droughts have also led to a decrease in water availability during the growing season, leading to low crop yields and food insecurity. The harsh winter conditions have also led to a higher risk of avalanches, landslides, and freezing temperatures, which affect the population's safety.

The government of Afghanistan has recognized the impacts of climate change and has initiated several projects to address them. The government has implemented reforestation projects and introduced drought-resistant crops to support the agriculture sector. Furthermore, the government has partnered with international organizations to improve the country's water system infrastructure and irrigation methods.

Conclusion

In conclusion, Afghanistan experiences diverse climatic zones, which affect the country's economy, agriculture, and social life. The country's climate pattern is arid, with low precipitation levels throughout the year. During winter and spring, the country experiences high winds and dust storms that affect the population's respiratory health. The weather patterns in Afghanistan include four distinct seasons, which bring varying weather conditions. The government has recognized the impacts of climate change and has initiated several projects to address them. However, more needs to be done to support the agricultural sector, improve infrastructure, and reduce the impacts of extreme weather events.

4. Quiz

1. Which of the following is a landlocked country in South Asia?

A. Nepal
   B. Bhutan
   C. Afghanistan
   D. All of the above

2. What is the capital city of Afghanistan?

A. Kabul
   B. Tehran
   C. Islamabad
   D. Baghdad

3. Which of the following mountain ranges run through Afghanistan?

A. Himalayas
   B. Alps
   C. Karakoram
   D. Hindu Kush

4. What is the highest peak in Afghanistan?

A. K2
  B. Mount Everest
  C. Mount Kilimanjaro
  D. Noshaq

5. What is the official language of Afghanistan?

A. English
  B. Pashto
  C. French
  D. Spanish

6. Which of the following rivers flows through Afghanistan?

A. Indus
  B. Nile
  C. Euphrates
  D. Amu Darya

7. What is the climate of Afghanistan?

A. Tropical
  B. Arctic
  C. Subtropical

D. Continental

8. Which of the following is a major environmental issue in Afghanistan?

A. Deforestation
  B. Desertification
  C. Global warming
  D. Acid rain

9. Which country borders Afghanistan to the north?

A. India
  B. Iran
  C. Pakistan
  D. Tajikistan

10. What is the approximate population of Afghanistan?

A. 10 million
  B. 20 million
  C. 30 million
  D. 40 million

Answers:

1. D. All of the above
2. A. Kabul
3. D. Hindu Kush
4. D. Noshaq
5. B. Pashto
6. D. Amu Darya
7. D. Continental
8. B. Desertification
9. D. Tajikistan
10. C. 30 million

III. Demography and Culture

1. Population and ethnic diversity

Introduction

Afghanistan, officially recognized as the Islamic Republic of Afghanistan, is a landlocked country in South Asia. It is bordered by Pakistan to the east and south, Iran to the west, Turkmenistan, Uzbekistan, and Tajikistan to the north, and China to the northeast. Afghanistan is known for its turbulent history, which has been marked by war, political unrest, and foreign intervention. However, the country is home to a culturally diverse population and boasts significant ethnic diversity. This paper aims to explore the population and ethnic diversity of Afghanistan, with a particular focus on the country's major ethnic groups and minority populations.

Population of Afghanistan

As of 2021, Afghanistan has an estimated population of 39.8 million people. The country's population has grown significantly since the 1950s, when it was estimated to be around 8 million people. The increase in population can be attributed primarily to high birth rates and improvements in healthcare, nutrition, and sanitation. However, Afghanistan still has one of the highest infant mortality rates in the world, and life expectancy is relatively low compared to other countries in the region.

The population of Afghanistan is young, with an estimated 44.7% of the population under the age of 15. This has significant implications for the country's future, as these young people will eventually enter the workforce and contribute to the economy. However, the country faces significant challenges in terms of providing education, healthcare, and employment opportunities to its young population.

Ethnic Diversity in Afghanistan

Afghanistan is home to a rich and diverse range of ethnic groups, each with their own distinct customs, traditions, and languages. The largest ethnic group in Afghanistan is the Pashtuns, who make up around 42% of the population. Pashtuns are primarily concentrated in the eastern and southern regions of the country, with significant populations in Kabul and other major cities.

The second-largest ethnic group in Afghanistan is the Tajiks, who make up around 27% of the population. Tajiks are primarily concentrated in the northern and western regions of the country, including the cities of Kabul and Mazar-i-Sharif. Tajiks are also found in significant numbers in neighboring countries such as Tajikistan and Uzbekistan.

The Hazaras are the third-largest ethnic group in Afghanistan, comprising around 9% of the population. Hazaras are primarily concentrated in the central highlands of Afghanistan, including the provinces of Bamyan, Ghor, and Daykundi. The Hazaras are also known for their distinctive physical features and are believed to have Mongol ancestry.

Other significant ethnic groups in Afghanistan include the Uzbeks (9%), the Aimaks (4%), and the Turkmen (3%). There are also smaller populations of Baloch, Nuristanis, and other ethnic groups.

Minority Populations

Afghanistan has a number of minority populations, including religious minorities such as Hindus, Sikhs, and Christians. These groups are often marginalized and face significant discrimination and persecution, particularly in areas controlled by the Taliban.

Afghanistan also has a significant population of internally displaced persons (IDPs) and refugees, many of whom have been forced to flee their homes due to conflict and political instability. The United Nations High Commissioner for Refugees (UNHCR) estimates that there are around 2.6 million Afghan refugees living in neighboring countries such as Pakistan and Iran, while an additional 4.1 million people are internally displaced within Afghanistan.

Challenges and Opportunities

Afghanistan's population and ethnic diversity present both challenges and opportunities for the country. On the one hand, the country's diverse ethnic groups have historically been a source of tension and conflict, particularly during periods of political instability. The Soviet occupation of Afghanistan in the 1980s and the subsequent civil war saw ethnic tensions rise to the forefront, leading to widespread violence and displacement.

However, Afghanistan's diversity can also be a source of strength and resilience. The country's history is marked by a long tradition of cultural exchange, particularly along the Silk Road trade routes that once traversed the region. This has led to a rich cultural heritage that is reflected in the country's art, literature, music, and architecture.

In recent years, there have been efforts to promote greater social, economic, and political inclusion for minority populations in Afghanistan. The country's new constitution, adopted in 2004, recognizes the rights of all citizens, regardless of ethnicity or religion. There have also been efforts to increase the representation of minority groups in political and government institutions.

Conclusion

In conclusion, Afghanistan is a country with a rich and diverse population, comprising numerous ethnic groups and minority populations. While these differences have historically been a source of tension and conflict, there are also opportunities to promote greater inclusion and diversity. Through education, social and political reforms, and improved economic opportunities, Afghanistan can work towards creating a more inclusive and equitable society that values and celebrates its many different cultures and ethnic groups.

2. Languages and dialects

Introduction:

Afghanistan is a diverse country that has been influenced by various cultures and civilizations over the centuries. The official languages of Afghanistan are Dari and Pashto, which are Indo-European languages. However, Afghanistan is also home to a variety of other languages and dialects spoken by different ethnic groups living within the country. The linguistic diversity of Afghanistan is a testament to the country's rich and complex history. This paper explores the languages and dialects of Afghanistan, their historical context, social significance, and the challenges associated with language preservation.

Overview of Afghanistan's Languages and Dialects:

Afghanistan is linguistically diverse, with more than 50 languages spoken throughout the country. The two official languages are Dari and Pashto, which are spoken by approximately 80% and 50% of the population, respectively. Dari is a dialect of Persian, which is spoken in Iran, Tajikistan, and parts of Uzbekistan. Pashto, on the other hand, belongs to the Indo-Iranian branch of languages and is closely related to other Indo-Aryan languages such as Hindi and Nepali.

Apart from Dari and Pashto, other significant languages spoken in Afghanistan include Uzbek, Turkmen, Balochi, and Pashayi. Uzbek and Turkmen belong to the Turkic language family, while Balochi is an Iranian language. Pashayi, on the other hand, is a language of the Nuristani group, which is unique to Afghanistan. Other minority languages spoken in Afghanistan include Arabic, Hindi, Urdu, and English.

Historical Context of Afghanistan's Languages and Dialects:

Afghanistan's linguistic diversity is a reflection of its complex and varied history. The country has been invaded and ruled by various external powers, including Alexander the Great, the Mauryan Empire, the Mongols, the Timurids, and the Mughals. The influence of these external powers has left a lasting impact on Afghanistan's culture and language.

The Persian influence on Afghanistan's language can be traced back to the 9th century when the Persian Samanid dynasty ruled over the region. The Persian language, which was the language of court and administration, gradually became the language of the educated elite and the literary language of Afghanistan. The Afghan monarchy, which ruled from the 18th century until the overthrow of King Zahir Shah in 1973, favored Persian as the language of administration and court. As a result, the use of Persian in Afghanistan's official spheres and literary works grew significantly.

The Pashto language also has its historical roots in Afghanistan. It was the language of the Pashtun tribes who dominated the southern regions of the country. The Pashtuns' influence on Afghanistan's history can be traced back to the 16th century when the Pashtun King Sher Shah Suri ruled over the region. Pashto became the language of administration during the reign of the Durrani Empire in the 18th century. Today, Pashto is widely spoken in southern Afghanistan, especially in Kandahar and Helmand provinces, and is the mother tongue of the majority of the Taliban.

The languages spoken by other ethnic groups in Afghanistan have also been influenced by external powers. Uzbek and Turkmen, for instance, were influenced by the Turkic migrations in the 11th and 12th centuries. Balochi, on the other hand, was influenced by the Baloch migration from Iran in the 17th and 18th centuries.

Social Significance of Languages and Dialects in Afghanistan:

The linguistic diversity of Afghanistan has both positive and negative social consequences. On the one hand, it creates a rich cultural heritage that is unique to the country. Each language and dialect has its own customs, traditions, folklore, and literature, adding to the country's cultural richness.

On the other hand, linguistic diversity can also fuel ethnic and linguistic tensions. Afghanistan's diverse ethnic groups are often divided along linguistic and cultural lines, which can lead to conflict. For instance, Pashto has been historically associated with dominance and power, which has led to resentment among other ethnic groups. Similarly, Dari speakers have often been associated with the intellectual and commercial elite, leading to resentment among Pashtuns.

In addition, the use of different languages and dialects in Afghanistan's official spheres has led to challenges in communication and administration. The use of Dari in official spheres has led to exclusion of Pashto speakers, while the use of Pashto has marginalized Dari speakers. The lack of language policies and standardization has made communication and administration more challenging, particularly in rural areas where many dialects are spoken.

Preservation of Languages and Dialects in Afghanistan:

The preservation of Afghanistan's linguistic diversity is crucial to preserving the country's cultural heritage. However, the task of language preservation is not without challenges. Languages and dialects in Afghanistan are at risk of extinction due to various factors, including urbanization, modernization, and political instability.

Urbanization and modernization have led to the displacement of rural communities, who are often the custodians of Afghanistan's minority languages and dialects. Many young people are migrating to urban centers, where they are exposed to different languages and cultures. As a result, there is a growing trend of language shift among younger generations, who are abandoning their mother tongue in favor of more dominant languages.

Political instability in Afghanistan has also posed a threat to Afghanistan's linguistic diversity. The ongoing conflict has led to the displacement of millions of people, many of whom have been forced to abandon their languages and dialects to assimilate into new communities.

Efforts to preserve Afghanistan's linguistic diversity have primarily been led by civil society organizations and NGOs. These organizations have been promoting language awareness and education, publishing literature in minority languages, and advocating for the use of minority languages in official spheres.

Conclusion:

Afghanistan's rich linguistic diversity is a testament to the country's complex and varied history. The country has been influenced by various cultures and civilizations throughout its history, which has led to the development of more than 50 languages and dialects. While this linguistic diversity has contributed to the country's cultural richness, it has also posed challenges to communication and administration.

The preservation of Afghanistan's linguistic diversity is crucial to preserving the country's cultural heritage. However, this task is not without challenges. Urbanization, modernization, and political instability all pose a threat to Afghanistan's linguistic diversity. Efforts by civil society organizations and NGOs to promote language awareness and education, publish literature in minority languages, and advocate for the use of minority languages in official spheres are critical in preserving and promoting Afghanistan's linguistic diversity.

3. Religion and beliefs

Religion and beliefs hold immense significance in Afghanistan, shaping its society, culture, and politics. As a predominantly Muslim nation, religion influences virtually every aspect of life in Afghanistan, from daily interaction to government policy to conflict resolution. Afghanistan's religious landscape is incredibly diverse and complex, with Sunni Islam being the dominant force, followed by Shia Islam, Sufi mysticism, and smaller religious minorities such as Bahá'í, Hindus, and Sikhs. This essay will delve into the intricacies of Afghanistan's religious landscape and the impact of religion and beliefs on various aspects of Afghan society.

Islam in Afghanistan

Islam is the predominant religion in Afghanistan, practiced by around 99% of the population. The majority of Afghan Muslims are Sunni, adhering to the Hanafi school of jurisprudence. However, a significant minority of Afghan Muslims are Shia, primarily belonging to the Twelver sect. The religious beliefs of the Afghan people are deeply intertwined with their culture, traditions, and daily life, making it challenging to separate religion from other aspects of Afghan society.

Islam has played a significant role in Afghanistan's history, culture, and identity, with the religion being instrumental in resistance and liberation movements, political movements, and the formation of social norms and values. Today, Islam continues to impact Afghan society in various ways, including political governance, conflict resolution, access to education and healthcare, and gender relations.

Political Governance in Afghanistan

Islam plays a prominent role in political governance in Afghanistan, with the country being an Islamic Republic. The Constitution of Afghanistan mandates that "no law shall contravene the tenets and provisions of the holy religion of Islam," with Islamic law serving as the ultimate source of legislation. The governing structure of Afghanistan reflects an appreciation for Islamic principles, with religious scholars and leaders having considerable influence over political decision-making.

The practice of Islamic law, also known as Shari'a, is a crucial aspect of political and legal governance in Afghanistan. The country has two judicial systems: the formal judicial system and the informal judicial system. The formal judicial system utilizes state-created laws and regulations, whereas the informal judicial system relies on traditional and religious practices for dispute resolution. The informal judicial system is common in rural and remote areas of Afghanistan where access to formal judicial systems is limited. Religious leaders play a crucial role in the informal judicial system, mediating disputes and offering guidance on legal and social matters.

Conflict Resolution and Peacebuilding

Religion has a vital role to play in conflict resolution and peace-building in Afghanistan. The country has been mired in conflict for decades, with religion often a root cause and a tool for the warring factions. Religious leaders have been influential in negotiating peace treaties and resolving disputes between conflicting parties. In Afghanistan's traditional tribal society, religious leaders play a significant role in mediating conflict and offering guidance on how to resolve disputes.

At the national level, Afghanistan's religious leaders have been instrumental in promoting peace and advocating for an end to violence. The Afghan Peace and Reintegration Program, launched in 2010, is an example of religious leaders playing a pivotal role in peacebuilding efforts. The program aimed to encourage Taliban insurgents to lay down their arms and reintegrate into Afghan society by offering them religious guidance and counseling by religious scholars. The peacebuilding process in Afghanistan is complex and multifaceted, with religion and beliefs playing a critical role in the process.

Access to Education and Healthcare

Religion also plays a role in access to education and healthcare in Afghanistan. Despite progress made towards improving access to education and healthcare in the country, disparities remain, particularly for girls and women. Afghanistan has some of the lowest literacy rates in the world, with only an estimated 38% of the population able to read and write. According to UNICEF, girls' enrollment in primary education is around 45%, significantly lower than boys' enrollment at 69%.

Religious leaders have been vocal in advocating for increased access to education and healthcare, particularly for girls and women. However, conservative beliefs and traditional practices in some areas of Afghanistan remain a barrier to girls' education and women's participation in the workforce. Conservative interpretations of Islamic teachings often view women's participation in public life, education, and healthcare as a threat to traditional gender roles and values.

Gender Relations

Religion and belief systems in Afghanistan play a significant role in shaping gender relations, with traditional gender roles being deeply rooted in Islamic principles and cultural values. The country's conservative social norms often limit women's mobility, autonomy, and participation in public life.

Under Taliban rule, women faced severe restrictions, including being required to wear the burqa in public, being barred from leaving the house without a male guardian, and being prohibited from attending school and working outside the home. Since the fall of the Taliban regime in 2001, women's rights in Afghanistan have improved, particularly in urban areas. However, discriminatory practices and violence against women persist in some parts of the country.

Religious leaders in Afghanistan have been vocal in promoting gender equality and advocating for women's rights. However, traditional attitudes towards gender roles and women's place in society remain significant barriers to progress. The role of religion and beliefs in shaping gender relations in Afghanistan is a complex and divisive issue, with religious leaders often holding conservative views that limit women's rights, particularly in rural areas.

Minority Religions in Afghanistan

Despite being a predominantly Muslim nation, Afghanistan is home to diverse religious and ethnic communities, each with its own set of beliefs, practices, and traditions. The Bahá'í faith, which originated in Iran, has a small but active community in Afghanistan. Hindus, Sikhs, and other religious minorities have traditionally played an important role in Afghan society, particularly in trade and economic activities. However, the rise of Islamist extremism in the country has placed these communities at risk, with many facing persecution, discrimination, and violence.

In conclusion, religion and beliefs in Afghanistan are deeply entwined with the country's society, culture, and politics. Islam's dominant role has been instrumental in shaping governance, conflict resolution, access to education and healthcare, gender relations, and the treatment of religious minorities. The impact of religion and beliefs on Afghan society is complex, with often competing interpretations of Islamic teachings and traditional cultural values. The role of religious leaders in promoting peace, advocating for women's rights, and protecting religious minorities is crucial for Afghanistan's future development and stability.

4. Social customs and practices

Introduction

Afghanistan is a country in South Asia, lying to the east of Iran, south of Turkmenistan, Uzbekistan and Tajikistan, and north of Pakistan. It is an Islamic country with a unique culture, traditions and social practices that have evolved over the centuries. Afghanistan has been subjected to various invasions and conflicts throughout history which have greatly influenced their customs and practices. The social customs and practices of Afghanistan are deeply rooted in religion, tribal affiliations, and cultural norms. In this essay, we will explore the social customs and practices of Afghanistan in relation to their history, religion, and cultural practices.

Afghanistan History

Afghanistan has a rich cultural and historical heritage that dates back to the Indus Valley Civilization, which existed between 2600 BC and 1900 BC. The region was conquered by the Persians in 550 BC, and Alexander the Great conquered most of Afghanistan in the 4th century BC. In the 7th century AD, Islam was introduced to Afghanistan when Arab armies invaded the region. In the 19th century, the British invaded Afghanistan several times, and the country became an independent nation in 1919.

During the Soviet-Afghan War in the 1980s, Afghanistan was invaded by the Soviet Union. This conflict led to a long and devastating civil war that lasted until 1996 when the Taliban took control of Afghanistan. Under the Taliban's rule, Afghanistan was subjected to harsh and oppressive laws that restricted many aspects of daily life. This period also saw the destruction of many of Afghanistan's cultural monuments and historical artifacts.

Following the U.S. invasion in 2001, Afghanistan has seen numerous challenges and conflicts that have impacted its society and culture. Despite this, many Afghans have maintained their traditions and customs, which continue to shape their daily lives.

Religion in Afghanistan

Islam plays a central role in the social customs and practices in Afghanistan. About 99% of Afghans practice Islam, which is divided into two main branches: Sunni and Shia. While there is a smaller percentage of minorities such as Hindus, Sikhs, and Christians, they are only allowed to practice their religions in private.

Islamic customs and beliefs influence many aspects of life in Afghanistan, from how people dress to how they interact with others. For example, Islamic law regulates the behavior between genders, with women often required to wear hijab (modest clothing) when in public. Men are also expected to dress modestly, with most opting for traditional Afghan clothing.

Muslims must observe five daily prayers and fast during the month of Ramadan. During Ramadan, Muslims are expected to abstain from food and drink from dawn until sunset. This fasting is considered a cleansing of the body and soul and is an essential part of the Islamic faith.

Family, Marriage and Gender Roles

Family is a central part of Afghan culture, with extended family members often living together in one household. The head of the family or "padar" plays an important role in decision-making and problem-solving for the family.

Marriage is an essential part of Afghan culture, and arranged marriages are still common, especially in rural areas. Parents often choose their children's partners, taking into consideration factors such as family background, education, and socioeconomic status. Marriages are often seen as a way to strengthen ties between families and tribes.

In traditional Afghan culture, women are expected to bear children and manage household duties. Men are often the sole providers for the family and are tasked with finding work to support their families financially. Gender roles in Afghanistan are quite rigid, and women are typically not allowed to have jobs outside of the home.

Education and Literacy

Education is an essential component of Afghan culture, and it is valued as a means to improve one's socioeconomic status. However, access to education is still a significant challenge in Afghanistan, particularly for women and girls. Despite efforts to increase education opportunities for girls, many are still not allowed to attend school due to cultural norms and traditions.

Literacy in Afghanistan is also an issue. According to the United Nations, the adult literacy rate in Afghanistan is only 43%, with women accounting for a significant percentage of the illiterate population.

Hospitality and Food

Hospitality is a cultural cornerstone of Afghanistan, and guests are treated with utmost respect and honor. Guests are often offered a cup of tea upon their arrival and are provided with the best possible accommodations and meals. Tea is the most popular beverage in Afghanistan and is served at nearly every social gathering.

Afghan cuisine is a blend of the region's various histories and cultures, with influences from Persia, India, and Central Asia. Rice, barley, and wheat are staples of the Afghan diet, often paired with meat or beans.

Spices such as cardamom, cumin, and coriander are also commonly used in Afghan cuisine.

Music and Dance

Music and dance are an essential part of Afghan culture, with traditional music and dance still widely popular today. The rubab, a traditional musical instrument, is often used in Afghan music, along with the tabla, a type of drum.

Afghanistan is also known for its traditional dance forms, such as the Attan, a group dance that is often performed at weddings and other social events. The Attan involves a series of fast-paced and repetitive steps, often accompanied by live music.

Conclusion

Afghanistan is a country with a unique and rich cultural heritage that has been shaped by its history, religion, and various conflicts. Islam plays a central role in the social customs and practices in Afghanistan, influencing everything from dress codes to gender roles. Family, hospitality, and education are also essential components of Afghan culture, while traditional music and dance continue to play a significant role in the country's social life. Despite many challenges, Afghans remain proud of their culture and traditions, which continue to shape the country's identity.

5. Quiz

1. What is the population of Afghanistan?
   a. 15 million
   b. 30 million
   c. 38 million
   d. 50 million

2. What is the official language of Afghanistan?
   a. Pashto
   b. Dari
   c. Hazaragi
   d. All of the above

3. What is the dominant religion in Afghanistan?
   a. Buddhism
   b. Zoroastrianism
   c. Islam
   d. Hinduism

4. What is the literacy rate in Afghanistan?
   a. 25%
   b. 43%
   c. 62%
   d. 81%

5. What is the life expectancy in Afghanistan?

a. 50 years
b. 60 years
c. 70 years
d. 80 years

6. Which of the following is a popular traditional Afghan dish?
    a. Sushi
    b. Pizza
    c. Qabuli palau
    d. Biryani

7. What is the traditional dress for men in Afghanistan?
    a. Bow tie and suit
    b. Kurta and shalwar kameez
    c. Jeans and t-shirts
    d. Tuxedo

8. What is the traditional form of music in Afghanistan?
    a. Rock music
    b. Hip-hop music
    c. Classical music
    d. Afghan folk music

9. What is the traditional form of dance in Afghanistan?
    a. Ballet
    b. Salsa
    c. Bhangra
    d. Attan

15

10. What is the national emblem of Afghanistan?
    a. Lion
    b. Eagle
    c. Sun
    d. Tulip

Answers:
    1. c. 38 million
    2. d. All of the above
    3. c. Islam
    4. b. 43%
    5. a. 50 years
    6. c. Qabuli palau
    7. b. Kurta and shalwar kameez
    8. d. Afghan folk music
    9. d. Attan
    10. c. Sun

IV. Politics and Governance

1. System of government

Introduction

Afghanistan is a landlocked country located in South Asia. It shares borders with Pakistan, Iran, Turkmenistan, Uzbekistan, and Tajikistan. Afghanistan has a population of approximately 38 million people, and it is made up of several ethnic groups. The country has a long and complex history, and its political system has been shaped by a variety of factors, including religion, culture, and external influences. The purpose of this paper is to discuss the system of government in Afghanistan, including its history, structure, and key issues facing the country today.

History of Government in Afghanistan

The history of government in Afghanistan dates back to the 18th century when the Pashtun leader, Ahmad Shah Durrani, established the Durrani Empire. The empire was characterized by a centralized government that was led by a king who had absolute power. However, the empire eventually fragmented, and Afghanistan became a collection of small tribal entities.

In the late 19th century, Afghanistan was ruled by the monarchy, which was characterized by a weak central government and powerful tribal leaders. The monarchy remained in power until 1973 when Mohammed Daoud Khan, the prime minister, staged a coup and declared himself president. He abolished the monarchy and replaced it with a republican system of government.

The Republican era was short-lived as it was characterized by political instability, unrest, and factionalism. In 1978, a group of Soviet-backed Communists seized power in a coup and established a Marxist-Leninist government. The government was opposed by the Mujahideen, a coalition of various Islamic and tribal groups.

The Mujahideen waged a protracted war against the Soviet-backed government, which lasted for over a decade. The conflict resulted in the collapse of the Communist government, and the establishment of the Islamic Republic of Afghanistan in 1992. However, the new government was greeted with internal conflict, and the country descended into civil war.

In 1996, the Taliban, a fundamentalist Islamic group, seized power in Kabul and established the Islamic Emirate of Afghanistan. The Taliban imposed strict Islamic law and were recognized by only a few countries, including Pakistan and Saudi Arabia. The Taliban was overthrown in 2001 following the US-led invasion, and the country returned to a system of democratic governance.

Structure of Government

The current system of government in Afghanistan is a democratic republic. The government is made up of three branches: the executive branch, the legislative branch, and the judicial branch.

The Executive Branch

The executive branch is led by the president, who is both the head of state and the head of government. The president is elected for a term of five years and can serve a maximum of two terms. The president appoints the cabinet, which is made up of ministers who are responsible for running the various government departments.

The Legislative Branch

The legislative branch is made up of two houses: the House of Representatives and the Senate. The House of Representatives, also known as the Wolesi Jirga, is made up of 250 members who are elected for a term of five years. The Senate, also known as the Meshrano Jirga, is made up of 102 members who are elected for a term of six years.

The Judicial Branch

The judicial branch is made up of a Supreme Court, which is the highest court in the country, and several lower courts. The Supreme

Court is made up of nine justices who are appointed by the president for a term of ten years.

Key Issues Facing the Government

The system of government in Afghanistan faces several key issues that have hampered its effectiveness and stability. One of the main issues is corruption, which is rampant at all levels of government. Corruption has undermined public trust in the government and has hindered the government's ability to provide basic services to its citizens.

Another key issue is the security situation in the country. Afghanistan has been plagued by conflict for decades, and despite efforts to establish peace, violence and instability persist. The Taliban remains a major threat, and the group has continued to carry out attacks on government forces and civilians.

Thirdly, ethnic and sectarian tensions have also been a major issue in Afghanistan's system of government. The country is made up of several ethnic groups, including Pashtuns, Tajiks, Hazaras, and Uzbeks, among others. The ethnic divisions have been exacerbated by political and economic disparities, and this has fueled conflicts and political instability.

Conclusion

In conclusion, the system of government in Afghanistan has been shaped by the country's history, culture, and external influences. While the country has made significant progress towards establishing democratic governance, it continues to face several key challenges, including corruption, insecurity, and ethnic tensions. Addressing these challenges will require the government to work towards building trust, promoting inter-ethnic harmony, and improving governance across all levels of government.

2. Political parties and affiliations

Political parties and affiliations in Afghanistan have a long and tumultuous history. Afghanistan's political landscape is marked by a legacy of tribal and ethnic rivalries, external interventions, and a lack of strong democratic institutions. For much of the 20th century, Afghanistan was ruled by authoritarian regimes that suppressed political parties and opposition groups. However, with the fall of the Taliban regime in 2001, Afghanistan's political system underwent significant changes, including the emergence of new political parties and affiliations. In this paper, we will explore the history of political parties and affiliations in Afghanistan, their current state, and the challenges they face.

Historical Background

The history of modern political parties and affiliations in Afghanistan dates back to the early 20th century. The first political parties in Afghanistan were established in the 1920s during the reign of King Amanullah Khan, who introduced many economic, social, and political reforms. However, these parties were not able to gain significant political power due to tribal and ethnic tensions and the continuation of authoritarian governance.

In the 1950s, the People's Democratic Party of Afghanistan (PDPA) emerged as a major political force. The PDPA was a Marxist-Leninist party that aimed to overthrow the monarchy and establish a socialist system in Afghanistan. The party gained significant support among the urban middle and working classes, but it faced strong opposition from conservative forces and rural tribal leaders.

In 1978, the PDPA launched a coup and established a communist regime with Nur Mohammad Taraki as the president. The regime implemented wide-ranging social, economic, and political reforms, but it faced massive resistance from various opposition groups, including Mujahideen fighters, who fought against the Soviet and Afghan government forces in the 1980s.

Political Parties and Affiliations Since 2001

Following the collapse of the Taliban regime in 2001, Afghanistan's political system underwent significant changes. A new constitution was drafted, and democratic institutions were put in place. Political parties and affiliations were allowed to operate legally and participate in elections. Afghanistan has a multi-party political system, with various political parties and affiliations operating across the country.

The Afghan political parties and affiliations are mainly divided along ethnic and tribal lines. The main ethnic groups are Pashtuns, Tajiks, Uzbeks, Hazaras, and Balochis. The two major political parties are the National Unity Movement (NUM) and the National Islamic Front of Afghanistan (NIFA). The NUM is dominated by Tajiks and draws support from other ethnic groups, whereas NIFA is dominated by the Pashtuns, the largest ethnic group in Afghanistan.

Other major political parties include the Islamic Society of Afghanistan, the Hizb-i-Wahdat, and the National Coalition of Afghanistan. There are also several smaller political parties and affiliations, including the Afghanistan Solidarity Party, the Afghanistan National Front, and the National Islamic Movement of Afghanistan.

Challenges Faced by Political Parties and Affiliations

Despite the significant progress made in Afghanistan's political system since 2001, political parties and affiliations face several challenges. One major challenge is the continued influence of tribal and ethnic politics. Afghanistan's political parties and affiliations are often seen as reflecting the interests of their respective ethnic or tribal group, rather than the broader interests of the country.

Another challenge is the lack of political cohesion and stability. Afghanistan has experienced regular political instability, with several regimes being overthrown or collapsing. Political parties and affiliations have not been able to establish strong coalitions and alliances, which has led to weak governance and a lack of effective policy implementation.

Another significant challenge is the continued presence of violent opposition groups, including Taliban and the Islamic State of Iraq and Syria (ISIS). These groups have consistently targeted political parties and affiliations, with several high-profile attacks on their offices and leaders. The presence of violent opposition groups has also made the holding of free and fair elections challenging.

Conclusion

Political parties and affiliations have a critical role to play in Afghanistan's democratic development. However, their efforts have been complicated by the country's complex history, tribal and ethnic rivalries, and external interventions. While significant progress has been made since 2001, there are still several challenges that need to be addressed, including entrenched ethnic and tribal politics, political instability, and violent opposition groups.

To address these challenges, political parties and affiliations will need to work towards building stronger coalitions and alliances that transcend ethnic and tribal lines. They will also need to strengthen their political institutions, establish cohesive policy platforms, and promote the rule of law and democratic values. By doing so, political parties and affiliations can contribute to a stable and democratic Afghanistan.

3. Foreign policy and relations

Introduction

The issue of foreign policy and relations is critical for Afghanistan, given its historical position as a strategic geopolitical location. From ancient times, Afghanistan has been a contested region, with major empires vying for control, including Alexander the Great, the Mongol Empire, and even the British Empire during the 19th and early 20th centuries. During the 20th century, Afghanistan experienced a tumultuous sequence of events, including the Soviet invasion, the rise of the Taliban, and the US-led coalition invasion in 2001. These events have had a profound impact on the foreign relations and policies of Afghanistan, as well as the country's economic, social, and political stability. This paper will examine the foreign policies and relationships that have shaped Afghanistan's history, including the challenges and opportunities that the country faces today.

The Soviet Invasion

One of the most significant geopolitical events that shaped Afghan foreign policy was the Soviet invasion of Afghanistan in 1979. For several months, the Soviet Union had been providing military and financial aid to the Afghan government, which was a member of the Soviet-led Warsaw Pact. However, as tensions escalated, the Soviet Union decided to launch a full-scale invasion to maintain its influence in the region. The invasion sparked a long and bloody conflict that lasted for over a decade, causing widespread destruction and destabilizing the entire region.

The Soviet invasion had a significant impact on foreign policy and relations in Afghanistan. Historically, Afghanistan had been a neutral state that had maintained a careful balance between East and West. The Soviet invasion led to a significant shift in this position, as the country became a battleground for the Cold War between the Soviet Union and the West. The Soviet invasion also led to the United States, Saudi Arabia, and Pakistan providing significant amounts of financial and military aid to the Afghan resistance groups, known as the Mujahideen. This aid had a profound impact on the conflict, as it enabled the Mujahideen to continue their resistance against the Soviet-backed government.

The Soviet invasion highlighted the importance of security and stability in Afghanistan for foreign policy and relationships. The conflict demonstrated the significant influence that external powers could exert on the country's internal affairs, leading to a significant shift in Afghanistan's relationships with its neighbors and traditional allies. The country also became a hotbed of extremism and terrorism, as extremist groups such as al-Qaida and the Taliban began to flourish in the chaos of the war. These groups have since become key factors in Afghanistan's current foreign policy and relationships.

The Rise of the Taliban

Following the withdrawal of Soviet troops in 1989, Afghanistan was left in a state of political and social chaos, and the country was increasingly under the control of various militias and warlords. The Taliban, which originated from a militant group that formed in 1994 to fight against Afghan warlords, gradually took control of much of the country by the late 1990s. The Taliban's rise to power was facilitated by the support of external actors, including Pakistan and Saudi Arabia.

The Taliban government had a significant impact on foreign policy and relationships in Afghanistan. The group implemented a strict interpretation of Islamic law, which led to diplomatic isolation and criticism from the international community. The Taliban's treatment of women, minorities, and political opponents was a major concern for many countries. The Taliban government also allowed al-Qaida to establish a large presence in the country, culminating in the 9/11 terrorist attacks in the United States.

The US-Led Coalition Invasion

In response to the 9/11 attacks, the United States led a coalition invasion of Afghanistan in 2001, with the aim of removing the Taliban government and destroying al-Qaida. The invasion was successful in achieving these objectives, and the Taliban was overthrown within a few months. However, the country was left without a functioning government, and the invasion led to significant social and political instability in Afghanistan. Additionally, the US-led coalition invasion resulted in the deaths of thousands of Afghan civilians, leading to significant anti-American sentiment within the country.

The US-led coalition invasion had a significant impact on foreign policy and relationships in Afghanistan. The invasion led to the formation of a new government, with significant Western support, which has been in power since 2002. The invasion also led to the integration of Afghanistan into the international community, with increased economic and political ties with major powers such as the United States, Europe, and China.

However, the US-led coalition invasion also had significant negative consequences for Afghan foreign policy and relationships. The invasion damaged relations with neighboring countries, including Pakistan and Iran, which have been accused of supporting the Taliban insurgency. There is also significant dissatisfaction among Afghans regarding the current government, which is seen as corrupt and lacks legitimacy. The ongoing instability and violence in the country have also placed significant pressure on neighboring countries, particularly Pakistan.

The Challenges Facing Afghan Foreign Policy and Relationships

Afghanistan faces significant challenges to maintaining stable foreign policy and relationships. These challenges stem from the country's internal instability, the ongoing presence of extremist groups, and its problematic relationship with neighboring countries.

One of the main challenges facing Afghanistan is the ongoing conflict with the Taliban. Despite significant international efforts to combat the group, the Taliban remains a significant force in the country, controlling large swaths of territory and launching regular attacks on government and civilian targets. The Taliban insurgency has also led to a significant increase in violence and instability in the country, negatively affecting foreign policy and relationships with neighboring countries.

Another challenge is Afghanistan's problematic relationship with neighboring countries, particularly Pakistan. The relationship between Afghanistan and Pakistan has been characterized by a history of conflict and tension, with Pakistan being accused of providing support to the Taliban insurgency. Iran is also active in Afghanistan, supporting various ethnic groups and providing financial support to the Taliban. These tensions have significantly impacted foreign policy and relationships for Afghanistan, with a lack of trust and cooperation between the countries.

Finally, Afghanistan also faces significant economic challenges that impact its foreign policy and relationships. The country is one of the poorest in the world, with over 54% of the population living below the poverty line. A lack of economic opportunities and infrastructure has led to an exodus of skilled workers and brain drain from the country, which negatively affects foreign policy and relationships. The country relies on aid from foreign countries, which can leave it vulnerable to external pressure and influence.

Conclusion

In conclusion, foreign policy and relationships are critical issues for Afghanistan, given its strategic geopolitical location and history of conflict with external powers. The Soviet invasion, the rise of the Taliban, and the US-led coalition invasion, have all had a significant impact on the country's foreign policy and relationships. Afghanistan faces significant challenges, including ongoing conflict with the Taliban, problematic relationships with neighboring countries, and economic instability. Addressing these challenges will require a coordinated international response, with significant investment in infrastructure, economic development, and combating extremism. By addressing these challenges, Afghanistan can become a stable, prosperous, and diplomatic member of the international community.

4. Human rights and freedoms

Introduction

Afghanistan is a country located in the central and southern parts of Asia, bordered by Pakistan, Iran, Turkmenistan, Uzbekistan, and Tajikistan. The country has had a tumultuous history of invasions, wars, and internal conflicts that have had a profound impact on its people's human rights and freedoms. After the fall of the Taliban, the US-led coalition tried to establish a democratic government and bring freedom and human rights to the Afghan people. However, 20 years later, Afghanistan is still grappling with issues of human rights violations, freedom of expression, and democracy.

This paper aims to look at the human rights and freedoms situation in Afghanistan, from the country's historical context to its current state. It will examine the various ways in which human rights are being violated and how ethnic and gender inequalities have contributed to these violations. The paper will also analyze the role of international organizations in promoting human rights in Afghanistan.

History of Afghanistan

Afghanistan has a rich and diverse history, dating back thousands of years. The country has been invaded multiple times by foreign powers, including the Persians, Greeks, Mongols, Mughals, and British. The invasions have shaped Afghanistan's history and culture, but they have also had a profound impact on the country's human rights situation.

In the 1970s, Afghanistan had a progressive government that was implementing various reforms, including providing education to women and promoting social welfare. However, in 1978, a coup d'état led by the Afghan Communist Party overthrew the government, leading to a decade-long civil war. During this period, human rights violations were rampant, with both sides committing atrocities against civilians.

In the 1990s, the Taliban rose to power, bringing with them a strict interpretation of Islamic law. Under the Taliban, human rights violations skyrocketed, and women were stripped of their rights and freedoms. When the US-led coalition toppled the Taliban in 2001, there was hope that Afghanistan could finally become a democracy that respects human rights and freedoms.

Freedom of Expression in Afghanistan

Freedom of expression is a fundamental human right that is enshrined in the constitution of Afghanistan. However, in reality, this right is often curtailed, especially when it comes to the media. Journalists and social media influencers have been targeted by both the government and extremist groups, leading to an environment of fear and self-censorship.

One of the most significant threats to freedom of expression in Afghanistan comes from extremist groups like the Taliban and ISIS. These groups have targeted journalists and media workers, often abducting or killing them. In 2018, a suicide bomber killed nine journalists in Kabul, including the well-known AFP photographer Shah Marai.

The government has also been accused of suppressing dissenting voices. In 2017, the government banned the popular messaging service WhatsApp, claiming that it was being used by the Taliban to communicate. However, many people believe that the ban was an attempt to suppress dissenting voices and limit freedom of expression.

Women's Rights in Afghanistan

Women's rights have been a contentious issue in Afghanistan, with women historically being marginalized and denied basic rights and freedoms. Under the Taliban, women were not allowed to leave their homes without a male escort, were not allowed to work, and were not allowed to attend school.

After the Taliban fell, there was hope that women's rights would be restored, and progress has been made. For instance, women have been allowed to vote and can run for political office. However, women still face significant barriers, including discrimination, violence, and limited access to education and healthcare.

Violence against women is a significant problem in Afghanistan, with women often facing domestic abuse, forced marriages, and honor killings. The Afghan government has taken steps to address this issue, but progress has been slow, and cultural attitudes towards women remain a significant barrier.

Ethnic Minorities in Afghanistan

Afghanistan is ethnically diverse, with the Pashtuns being the largest ethnic group, followed by the Tajiks, Hazaras, and Uzbeks. Ethnic tensions have been a significant contributor to the country's instability, with different ethnic groups vying for power and influence.

Ethnic minorities in Afghanistan have historically faced discrimination and marginalization. During the Taliban era, ethnic minorities like the Hazaras were targeted, with many being killed or forced to flee the country. Even after the fall of the Taliban, ethnic minorities have continued to face discrimination, both from the government and extremist groups.

In recent years, there has been a rise in ethnic tensions in Afghanistan, with the Pashtuns and Hazaras clashing in several provinces. The Taliban have also targeted ethnic minorities, with reports of ethnic cleansing of the Hazaras in the province of Daikundi.

International Support for Human Rights in Afghanistan

The international community has played a significant role in supporting human rights in Afghanistan, especially after the fall of the Taliban. International organizations, such as the UN and its various agencies, have provided funding and technical assistance to improve the country's human rights situation.

The US-led coalition has also invested heavily in promoting human rights and democracy in Afghanistan. However, the effectiveness of these efforts has been called into question, with some arguing that the US focus on counterterrorism has come at the expense of promoting human rights and freedom.

Conclusion

The human rights and freedoms situation in Afghanistan is complex, with historical, cultural, and political factors contributing to the challenges faced by the Afghan people. While progress has been made in some areas, such as women's rights, there are still significant and pervasive violations of human rights in the country. The international community must continue to play a role in supporting human rights in Afghanistan and promoting a stable and peaceful society.

5. Quiz

1. What type of government does Afghanistan currently have?
  A. Absolute monarchy
  B. Socialist republic
  C. Islamic republic
  D. Constitutional monarchy

Answer: C. Islamic republic

2. Who was the first president of Afghanistan after the fall of the Taliban regime?
  A. Hamid Karzai
  B. Ashraf Ghani
  C. Abdullah Abdullah
  D. Amrullah Saleh

Answer: A. Hamid Karzai

3. What is the name of the Lower House of the Afghan Parliament?
  A. Shura
  B. National Assembly
  C. Majlis
  D. Wolesi Jirga

Answer: D. Wolesi Jirga

4. What is the main source of revenue for the Afghan government?
    A. Agriculture
    B. Oil exports
    C. Mineral resources
    D. Foreign aid

Answer: D. Foreign aid

5. Which group governs the majority of the rural areas in Afghanistan?
    A. Taliban
    B. Islamic State (ISIS)
    C. Afghan National Army
    D. Afghan National Police

Answer: A. Taliban

6. What is the role of the Afghan Supreme Court?
    A. Executive power
    B. Legislative power
    C. Judicial power
    D. Military power

Answer: C. Judicial power

7. Who has the power to appoint the members of the Afghan Supreme Court?
    A. The president
    B. The parliament
    C. The Supreme Court itself
    D. The constitutional council

Answer: A. The president

8. What is the minimum age requirement to be elected to the Afghan Parliament?
    A. 18 years old
    B. 21 years old
    C. 25 years old
    D. 30 years old

Answer: C. 25 years old

9. What is the name of the National Security Advisor to the President of Afghanistan?
    A. Amrullah Saleh
    B. Abdullah Abdullah
    C. Hamdullah Mohib
    D. Ashraf Ghani

Answer: C. Hamdullah Mohib

10. What year did Afghanistan adopt its current constitution?
    A. 2001
    B. 2002
    C. 2003
    D. 2004

Answer: D. 2004

V. Economy and Development

1. Economic sectors and industries

Introduction

Afghanistan is a landlocked country in South Asia that is strategically located between the Middle East, Central Asia, and South Asia. It is bordered by Pakistan to the east and south, Iran to the west, Turkmenistan, Uzbekistan, and Tajikistan to the north, and China to the northeast. The country has a rich history and culture, but in recent times, it has been plagued by war, political instability, and economic challenges. However, with the establishment of a democratic government and the withdrawal of foreign troops, Afghanistan has the potential to capitalize on its strategic location and natural resources to develop its economy. This paper will explore the economic sectors and industries in Afghanistan.

Agriculture

Agriculture is the backbone of Afghanistan's economy, contributing approximately 24% of the country's gross domestic product (GDP) and employing about 80% of the population. The country has a vast agricultural potential due to its fertile land, water resources, and diverse climate. The most important agricultural products in Afghanistan include wheat, barley, maize, rice, fruits, and vegetables. In addition, the country is known for its high-quality saffron, pomegranate, and other dry fruits.

Despite the potential of agriculture, its growth has been hampered by several factors, including the lack of infrastructure, modern farming techniques, and access to markets. Moreover, Afghanistan's agriculture is highly dependent on rainwater, making it vulnerable to climate change and droughts. In recent years, the government has launched various initiatives to modernize agriculture, increase productivity, and access to markets. For instance, the National Agriculture Development Framework (NADF) aims to increase productivity, promote value chain development, and enhance access to finance and markets.

Mining

Afghanistan is rich in mineral resources, including gold, copper, iron ore, lithium, and rare earth elements. These resources are estimated to be worth over USD 1 trillion, making Afghanistan one of the wealthiest countries in the region. However, despite its vast mineral wealth, the country's mining sector remains largely untapped due to political instability, security challenges, and limited infrastructure.

In recent years, the government has taken steps to encourage foreign investment in the mining sector. For instance, the government has signed several mining contracts with foreign companies, including China, India, and the United States. In addition, the government has established a legal framework for the mining sector, including the Minerals Law (2018) and the Mining Regulations (2019). These laws aim to promote transparency, accountability, and sustainability in the mining sector.

Manufacturing

Manufacturing is another vital sector in Afghanistan, contributing approximately 17% of the country's GDP. The manufacturing sector includes textiles, food processing, chemical production, and construction materials. However, the manufacturing sector is relatively underdeveloped, and most of the goods are imported from neighboring countries.

The government has launched several initiatives to promote the manufacturing sector, including the "Made in Afghanistan" campaign, which aims to promote locally produced goods. In addition, the government is working to improve access to finance and develop infrastructure to support the manufacturing sector. Despite these initiatives, the manufacturing sector is still hampered by challenges such as inadequate infrastructure, limited access to credit, and a lack of skilled labor.

Services

The services sector is one of the fastest-growing sectors in Afghanistan, contributing approximately 52% of the country's GDP. The services sector includes trade, transport, telecommunications, finance, and tourism. The sector has benefited from the growth of the telecommunications industry, which has significantly improved access to mobile and internet services in the country.

The government has launched several initiatives to promote the services sector, including the National Export Strategy (NES), which aims to boost the country's exports and diversify its economy. In addition, the government is working to improve infrastructure and access to finance to support the services sector. However, the services sector is still hampered by challenges such as limited access to credit, poor infrastructure, and lack of skilled labor.

Energy

Energy is another critical sector in Afghanistan, which has significant potential for renewable energy, particularly solar and wind power. The country imports most of its energy needs, including oil and gas, from neighboring countries. However, the high cost of importing energy has had a significant impact on the country's economy.

In recent years, the government has taken steps to promote renewable energy, including the development of the Afghan National Renewable Energy Policy and Strategy. The policy aims to increase the share of renewable energy in the country's energy mix and leverage public-private partnerships to boost investment in the renewable energy sector.

Conclusions

In conclusion, Afghanistan is a country with vast potential in various economic sectors and industries. Agriculture remains the backbone of the country's economy, contributing significantly to the country's GDP and employing a significant portion of the population. However, the sector is still hindered by limited infrastructure, lack of access to markets, and vulnerability to climate change. The country's mineral resources provide significant potential for the development of the mining sector, although the sector is hampered by political instability and security challenges.

The manufacturing sector is relatively underdeveloped, and most of the country's goods are imported from neighboring countries. The services sector is the fastest-growing sector in the country, benefiting from the growth of the telecommunications industry. However, the sector is still hampered by limited access to credit, poor infrastructure, and lack of skilled labor. The energy sector provides significant potential for the development of renewable energy, although the sector is still dependent on imports.

Overall, to achieve sustainable economic growth and development, Afghanistan needs to address several challenges, including political instability, security challenges, and limited infrastructure. The government must continue to promote foreign investment and public-private partnerships to support economic growth and development. In addition, the government needs to develop policies and strategies that promote transparency, accountability, and sustainability in various economic sectors and industries.

2. Natural resources and exports

Introduction

Afghanistan is a landlocked country in South Asia, bordered by Pakistan, Iran, Turkmenistan, Uzbekistan, and Tajikistan. It is one of the poorest countries in the world, with high poverty rates, poor infrastructure, and limited access to basic services such as healthcare and education. This paper will focus on the relationship between natural resources, exports, and the economy of Afghanistan.

Natural Resources

Afghanistan is a country rich in natural resources such as iron ore, copper, gold, lithium, uranium, and rare earth elements. However, the country has been largely unable to capitalize on these resources due to a weak infrastructure, lack of investment, and ongoing conflict. The mining sector remains underdeveloped and is dominated by small-scale artisanal mining operations.

One of the most significant natural resources in Afghanistan is lithium, which is used in the production of batteries for electric cars, cellphones, and other electronic devices. According to the United States Geological Survey, Afghanistan holds one of the largest unexplored lithium deposits in the world, estimated to be worth over $1 trillion. However, the exploitation of lithium in Afghanistan is still in its early stages, and there are concerns about environmental impacts and the potential for the resource to exacerbate existing conflict in the country.

Another significant natural resource in Afghanistan is opium, produced from poppy cultivation. Afghanistan is the world's largest producer of opium, accounting for over 80% of the global production. Despite efforts by the Afghan government and international organizations to curb opium production, it remains a major source of income and livelihood for many Afghans. The production and sale of opium also contribute to corruption and violence in the country, as drug trafficking is often linked to armed groups and criminal networks.

Exports

Exports are an essential component of the Afghan economy, comprising over 30% of the country's GDP. The primary exports are natural gas, fresh and dried fruits, nuts, cotton, wool, and carpets. India, Pakistan, the United States, and Russia are the main export destinations.

Fruits and nuts are the largest export category, accounting for over 30% of total exports. Afghanistan is known for its high-quality dried fruits such as figs, apricots, and raisins, as well as fresh fruits such as pomegranates and melons. However, the export of fruits and nuts is subject to seasonal fluctuations and depends heavily on the infrastructure and logistics available for transportation and distribution.

Cotton is the second-largest export category, accounting for over 20% of total exports. Afghanistan has a long tradition of cotton production, and the crop is grown by small-scale farmers across the country. However, the cotton industry has faced challenges such as low prices, inadequate irrigation systems, and poor quality control, which have hindered its growth and development.

Natural gas is another significant export, primarily to neighboring Pakistan. The Amu Darya Basin in northern Afghanistan holds an estimated 160 billion cubic meters of natural gas, but the sector remains underdeveloped due to inadequate infrastructure and security concerns.

Challenges and Opportunities

Afghanistan's natural resources and exports face several significant challenges and opportunities. On the one hand, the country is rich in natural resources, and there is significant potential for investment and growth in the mining sector, especially with the demand for lithium increasing due to the growing electric car industry. On the other hand, the exploitation of natural resources can contribute to environmental degradation, exacerbate conflict, and deepen social inequalities, as seen with the opium industry.

The export sector also faces challenges, such as limited access to markets, inadequate infrastructure, and security concerns. However, there are opportunities for growth and development, especially in the agricultural sector, where Afghanistan has a comparative advantage in the production of high-quality fruits, nuts, and cotton. The government and international organizations can invest in infrastructure, logistics, and quality control to enhance the competitiveness of these products in global markets.

Conclusion

In conclusion, Afghanistan's natural resources and exports play a critical role in the country's economy, but there are significant challenges and opportunities to be addressed. The exploitation of natural resources must be done in a sustainable and equitable manner, while the export sector must be enhanced and diversified to reduce the country's dependence on a few products and markets. Achieving these goals will require cooperation between the government, private sector, and international organizations, as well as a stable and secure environment to attract investment and promote economic growth.

3. Investment and trade opportunities

Introduction

Afghanistan has faced numerous conflicts and challenges for decades, which disrupted its economy and social structure. The country, since 2001, has been working hard towards developing a stable, democratic government which can provide a conducive environment for business and economic growth. However, Afghanistan's economy remains fragile due to its reliance on foreign aid and traditional agricultural activities. The Afghan government and business community have been working towards expanding its economy by identifying investment and trade opportunities that will help create jobs, contribute to development, and reduce its dependence on aid. This paper will explore some of the investment and trade opportunities in Afghanistan.

Investment Opportunities

Agriculture

Agriculture forms the backbone of the Afghan economy, contributing approximately 22% of its GDP, employing 80% of its rural population and providing raw materials to its industries. Afghanistan has a wealth of untapped natural resources, including arable land that can support large-scale commercial farming. The country's fertile plains and valleys, combined with its ample water supply, present excellent opportunities for farmers and investors to invest in agriculture. The country can produce a wide range of crops such as apples, cherries, peaches, apricots, grapes, pomegranates, almonds, pistachios, and figs for local consumption and export purposes.

Apart from fruits and nuts, Afghanistan can also produce high-value crops such as saffron and medicinal herbs. Afghanistan produces about 90% of the world's saffron, making it one of the most lucrative crops for investment. Additionally, Afghanistan produces a large amount of wild and cultivated opiates, which could be used in the pharmaceutical industry as painkillers.

Infrastructure

Afghanistan's infrastructure is underdeveloped, which is a major constraint to trade, investment, and economic growth. The Afghan government, along with donor countries and international organizations, is investing in the country's infrastructure to create an enabling environment for businesses. The government has prioritized the construction of a railway network to connect the country to its neighboring countries, especially to Iran and China, which will improve the country's transportation and logistics system. Afghanistan also plans to build a network of highways, which will connect the country's provinces to the major trade routes, including the proposed Central Asia-South Asia electricity transmission and trade project. The country seeks investments in infrastructure development to boost economic growth, such as airport construction, housing, and water and sanitation projects.

Mining

Afghanistan is rich in minerals such as gold, copper, iron, lithium, and precious stones. Investing in the mining sector has the potential to drive economic development in Afghanistan. However, the sector must be developed in a transparent and accountable manner to ensure it benefits the country and its people. The government has developed a mining law to provide licenses and establish a legal framework for mining operations. The government has awarded several contracts to international mining companies, such as China Metallurgical Group and the Turkish consortium, to develop the Aynak copper mine and the Hajigak iron mine, respectively.

Tourism

Afghanistan has a unique cultural heritage and a stunning landscape that provides excellent tourism opportunities. The country has some of the world's most important cultural sites, such as the ancient city of Balkh, the Buddhas of Bamiyan, and Herat's Islamic architecture. The country is also home to the stunning scenery of the Hindu Kush mountain range and the Band-e-Amir National Park, which has become an increasingly popular tourist destination. While the security situation in Afghanistan is still fragile, the government is taking steps to improve the security situation to attract tourists.

Trade Opportunities

Energy

Afghanistan's energy sector is underdeveloped, but it has great potential for growth. The country has hydropower potential of over 23,000 MW and significant solar and wind resources. Energy consumption in Afghanistan is increasing rapidly due to population growth and urbanization, which has led to power shortages. The government has set ambitious targets to increase renewable energy sources' share in the country's energy mix, and they seek to attract investors to develop the energy sector.

Textiles and Clothing

Afghanistan has abundant, high-quality cotton that can support a local textile and clothing industry. The sector has the potential to provide many jobs and create economic growth. The Afghan government has implemented a cotton law to safeguard the quality and standard of its cotton production. The country also has a skilled and experienced workforce in the textile industry, making it an attractive investment destination.

Construction Materials

Afghanistan's construction industry has grown significantly since 2001, creating a high demand for construction materials. The country has the potential to become a significant supplier of construction materials such as marble, limestone, and cement. The construction materials sector has the potential to create job opportunities and local economic growth, particularly in rural areas. The Afghan government has initiated several infrastructure development projects that require local construction materials, providing an excellent opportunity for investors to tap into this market.

Challenges and Risks

Investors looking to do business in Afghanistan must consider the risks and challenges associated with the country. Although the Afghan government is implementing measures to support investment, the country still faces high levels of corruption, poor governance, and insecurity. The presence of extremist groups such as the Taliban, the Islamic State of Khorasan Province (ISKP), and Al Qaeda is a major concern due to their involvement in numerous attacks and bombings that have targeted innocent people and businesses. The security situation in the country remains volatile and unpredictable, which is a significant deterrent to investment.

Moreover, Afghanistan's weak legal and regulatory frameworks remain a challenge, causing uncertainty for investors. The country also faces infrastructure challenges, particularly in transport and logistics, which can be a costly and time-consuming issue. The country's bureaucratic processes and regulatory procedures also pose challenges to investors, particularly small and medium enterprises. Furthermore, the country's lack of diversification in its economy means that Afghanistan is still heavily reliant on imports, limiting revenue potential for local businesses.

Conclusion

Afghanistan has vast untapped investment and trade opportunities. Agriculture, mining, infrastructure, tourism, and energy present opportunities for both local and international investors. However, investing in Afghanistan has its risks and challenges, such as security concerns, weak regulatory frameworks, and infrastructure constraints. The Afghan government must work towards improving its business environment by enhancing governance, reducing corruption, and investing in the country's infrastructure. Tackling these issues will improve the country's attractiveness to investors, generating economic growth and contributing to poverty reduction.

4. Infrastructure and development plans

Introduction

Afghanistan is a landlocked, mountainous, and war-ravaged country in South Asia. It has historically been a crossroads of civilizations, cultures, and trade routes, from the Persian Empire to the Silk Road. However, Afghanistan has suffered from decades of conflict and instability, which have taken a heavy toll on its people, economy, and social fabric. The U.S.-led invasion in 2001 toppled the Taliban regime but failed to bring lasting peace or prosperity to Afghanistan. Despite some progress in security, governance, and development, the country remains fragile and vulnerable to violence, corruption, and poverty.

Infrastructure and development plans are critical to Afghanistan's future as a sovereign, stable, and prosperous state. Infrastructure refers to the physical and organizational systems, structures, and facilities that support economic, social, and political activities, such as roads, bridges, airports, ports, power grids, water supply, sanitation, health care, education, and communication. Development, on the other hand, encompasses the broader goals and strategies for improving people's lives and reducing poverty, inequality, and vulnerability, including economic growth, job creation, human capital, governance, and social services.

This paper provides an overview of the infrastructure and development plans in Afghanistan, their challenges and opportunities, and their implications for the country's future. The paper first reviews the

103

background and context of the infrastructure and development challenges in Afghanistan. It then analyzes the key strategies, programs, and projects that the Afghan government, donors, and partners have undertaken to address these challenges, focusing on the sectors of transportation, energy, water and sanitation, health, education, and governance. The paper also discusses the challenges and constraints that limit the effectiveness and sustainability of these efforts, including insecurity, corruption, capacity, and funding gaps. Finally, the paper concludes with some policy recommendations to enhance the impact and sustainability of the infrastructure and development plans in Afghanistan.

Background and Context

Afghanistan faces multiple and interconnected infrastructure and development challenges that stem from its geography, history, and conflicts. Afghanistan has a rugged terrain, which makes transportation and communication difficult, especially during the harsh winter season. It also has a low level of arable land and water resources, which affects its agriculture and food security. Afghanistan's population is predominantly rural, with high levels of poverty and illiteracy, and low levels of access to health care and education. Moreover, Afghanistan has been caught in a cycle of violence and instability, which has destroyed much of its infrastructure, disrupted its social cohesion, and undermined its governance and sovereignty.

The Soviet invasion of Afghanistan in 1979 marked the beginning of decades of conflict and violence that have ravaged the country's infrastructure and institutions. The Soviet occupation, which lasted until 1989, was resisted by various Afghan resistance groups, some of which were supported by the U.S. and its allies. The withdrawal of the Soviets led to a power vacuum and civil war, which eventually led to the establishment of the Taliban regime in 1996. The Taliban implemented a strict interpretation of Islam and imposed brutal measures on the population, including the ban on education for girls, the destruction of cultural heritage, and the harboring of foreign terrorist networks, such as Al-Qaeda. The U.S.-led invasion in 2001 aimed to topple the Taliban, capture or eliminate Al-Qaeda leaders, and establish a democratic and stable government. However, the war has dragged on for two decades and has claimed the lives of tens of thousands of Afghan civilians, soldiers, and insurgents, as well as thousands of U.S. and NATO troops.

The war has devastated Afghanistan's infrastructure and institutions, including its roads, bridges, airports, seaports, power plants, water systems, health centers, schools, and government buildings. The conflict has also uprooted millions of Afghans from their homes and communities, forcing them to become refugees, internally displaced persons, or migrants. The war has also bred corruption, criminality, and impunity, fueling a culture of greed, distrust, and injustice. Corruption has undermined the effectiveness and legitimacy of the Afghan government and has eroded public trust and support. Moreover, insecurity remains the major threat to Afghanistan's stability and development, as the Taliban and other insurgent groups continue to launch attacks, assassinations, and intimidation against civilians, government officials, and infrastructure facilities.

Strategies, Programs, and Projects

To address Afghanistan's infrastructure and development challenges, the Afghan government, donors, and partners have implemented various strategies, programs, and projects in the sectors of transportation, energy, water and sanitation, health, education, and governance. These initiatives aim to improve access, quality, and sustainability of services and infrastructure, as well as to promote economic growth, job creation, and social inclusion. Some of the key strategies, programs, and projects are discussed below.

Transportation

Transportation is critical to Afghanistan's development, as it connects people, goods, and services across the country and beyond. Afghanistan's road network, however, is underdeveloped, poorly maintained, and insecure, which limits mobility, trade, and investment. To improve Afghanistan's transportation infrastructure, the government and donors have launched the National Transport Plan (NTP) in 2016, which aims to enhance road, rail, air, and sea connectivity, as well as to promote regional integration and cooperation.

The NTP has prioritized the construction and rehabilitation of key highways and corridors, such as the Kabul-Kandahar-Herat Road, the Jalalabad-Torkham Road, and the Hairatan-Mazar-i-Sharif Railway, as well as the expansion and upgrading of regional airports and seaports. The NTP has also sought to improve the regulatory and institutional frameworks for transport management and safety, as well as to strengthen the capacities of the Ministry of Transport and Civil Aviation and other relevant agencies.

Energy

Energy is another critical sector for Afghanistan's development, as it provides power for homes, businesses, and industries, and fuels economic growth and social services. Afghanistan's energy sector, however, is underdeveloped and reliant on imports from neighboring countries, especially Iran and Turkmenistan. To address this challenge, the Afghan government and donors have launched the Afghanistan Energy Sector Master Plan (AESMP) in 2017, which aims to increase the domestic production and distribution of renewable and non-renewable energy sources, as well as to enhance energy efficiency and conservation.

The AESMP has proposed various projects and programs, such as the construction and operation of solar, hydro, wind, and thermal power plants, the expansion and upgrading of transmission and distribution networks, the promotion of private sector investment and public-private partnerships, and the improvement of regulatory and institutional frameworks for electricity pricing, tariffs, and subsidies. The AESMP has also emphasized the importance of regional energy cooperation and integration, especially with Central and South Asian countries, and the role of women and local communities in energy planning and management.

Water and Sanitation

Water and sanitation are basic human needs and fundamental rights, which are critical for public health, hygiene, and well-being. Afghanistan's water and sanitation systems, however, are underdeveloped, inadequate, and vulnerable to natural disasters and pollution. To address this challenge, the Afghan government and donors have launched the National Water Resource Strategy (NWRS) in 2017, which aims to improve access to safe and sustainable water sources and sanitation facilities, as well as to strengthen the capacity of the Ministry of Energy and Water and other relevant agencies.

The NWRS has identified various programs and projects, such as the construction and rehabilitation of irrigation networks, dams, and water treatment plants, the promotion of community-based approaches to water management and conservation, the enhancement of water governance and regulation, and the mainstreaming of water and sanitation considerations into national policies and plans. The NWRS has also emphasized the importance of gender and equity considerations in water and sanitation planning and management, as well as of regional water cooperation and diplomacy.

Health

Health is a basic human right and essential for human development and dignity. Afghanistan's health sector, however, is underdeveloped, fragile, and vulnerable to disease outbreaks and emergencies. To address this challenge, the Afghan government and donors have launched the Basic Package of Health Services (BPHS) in 2003 and the

Essential Package of Hospital Services (EPHS) in 2005, which aim to provide basic and essential health care services to all Afghan citizens, particularly women and children, and to strengthen the capacity of the Ministry of Public Health and other relevant agencies.

The BPHS and EPHS have provided various health services, such as primary care, maternal and child health, reproductive health, immunization, infectious diseases control, mental health, and emergency care. These services have been delivered through a network of health facilities, such as clinics, health posts, and hospitals, as well as through community health workers and outreach teams. The BPHS and EPHS have also emphasized the importance of gender and equity considerations in health planning and service delivery, as well as the integration of health with other sectors, such as nutrition, water and sanitation, and education.

Education

Education is an essential human right and critical for human development and empowerment. Afghanistan's education sector, however, is underdeveloped, inadequate, and vulnerable to insecurity and cultural barriers. To address this challenge, the Afghan government and donors have launched the National Education Strategic Plan (NESP) in 2017, which aims to provide quality education to all Afghan citizens, particularly girls and marginalized groups, and to strengthen the capacity of the Ministry of Education and other relevant agencies.

The NESP has proposed various programs and projects, such as the construction and rehabilitation of schools, teacher training, curriculum development, assessment and accreditation, and the promotion of community involvement and ownership in education. The NESP has also emphasized the importance of gender and equity considerations in education planning and service delivery, as well as the integration of education with other sectors, such as health, water and sanitation, and vocational training.

Governance

Governance is a critical factor for Afghanistan's development, as it provides the legal, institutional, and regulatory frameworks for responsible and accountable management and allocation of resources and services. Afghanistan's governance, however, is weak, corrupt, and fragmented, which undermines the effectiveness and legitimacy of the Afghan government, as well as the trust and support of the Afghan people. To address this challenge, the Afghan government and donors have launched various programs and projects, such as the National Priority Program (NPP) for Rule of Law and Justice, the Citizens' Charter Program (CCP), and the Anti-Corruption and Civil Service Reform programs.

The NPP aims to strengthen the judicial and legal systems, as well as to promote human rights and access to justice for all Afghan citizens, especially women and vulnerable groups. The CCP aims to provide basic and essential services to rural and urban communities, such as health, education, water and sanitation, and livelihood opportunities, through a participatory and decentralized approach. The

Anti-Corruption and Civil Service Reform programs aim to promote transparency, accountability, and merit-based recruitment and promotion of public servants, as well as to reduce corruption and improve public services delivery.

Challenges and Constraints

The infrastructure and development plans in Afghanistan face multiple and interconnected challenges and constraints that limit their effectiveness and sustainability. Some of these challenges and constraints are discussed below.

Insecurity

Insecurity is the major challenge to Afghanistan's infrastructure and development plans, as it undermines the safety, accessibility, and sustainability of services and infrastructure. The Taliban and other insurgent groups continue to launch attacks, assassinations, and intimidation against civilians, government officials, and infrastructure facilities, such as roads, bridges, airports, schools, and health centers. This insecurity affects not only the physical security of people and assets but also the psychological and social well-being of the Afghan population, as well as the perception of the Afghan government and its partners. Insecurity also reduces investors' confidence and increases the cost and risk of doing business in Afghanistan, which hinders economic growth and job creation.

Corruption

Corruption is the cancer that eats away at Afghanistan's infrastructure and development plans, as it undermines the transparency, accountability, and effectiveness of governance and public services. Corruption affects not only the financial resources and assets of the Afghan government and its partners but also the quality and availability of services and infrastructure. Corruption creates a culture of impunity and injustice, as well as a perception of mistrust and cynicism among the Afghan people. Corruption erodes public trust and support, which undermines the legitimacy and stability of the Afghan government and its partners. Corruption also reduces the attractiveness and competitiveness of Afghanistan as a destination for investment and aid, which reduces the long-term sustainability of the infrastructure and development plans.

Capacity

Capacity is the limit to Afghanistan's infrastructure and development plans, as it restricts the ability of the Afghan government and its partners to plan, design, implement, and monitor sustainable and effective investments and projects. Capacity gaps exist at various levels and sectors, such as policy-making, implementation, monitoring, and evaluation, as well as in the technical, institutional, and human resources domains. Capacity gaps also exist in the public, private, and civil society sectors, as well as in the regional and global arenas. Capacity-building requires long-term and sustained investments, as well as a systemic and coordinated approach that addresses the root causes and challenges of capacity limitations.

Funding

Funding is the constraint to Afghanistan's infrastructure and development plans, as it limits the resources and investments available for sustainable and effective projects and programs. Funding gaps exist in various forms and domains, such as budget deficits, donor fatigue, uncertainness, and prioritization. Funding gaps affect the quality and scope of services and infrastructure, as well as the sustainability and ownership of investments and projects. Funding gaps also create a dependency syndrome, as well as a perception of unfulfilled promises and expectations among the Afghan people. Funding requires a creative and innovative approach that seeks to mobilize and leverage resources from multiple sources and stakeholders, as well as to combine public and private investments and ownership.

Policy Recommendations

To enhance the impact and sustainability of Afghanistan's infrastructure and development plans, the following policy recommendations are proposed:

1. Prioritize security and stability as the precondition for effective and sustainable development.

2. Strengthen governance and anti-corruption measures as the foundation for responsible and accountable management and allocation of resources and services.

3. Invest in capacity building and institutional strengthening as the basis for planning, designing, implementing, and monitoring sustainable and effective projects and investments.

4. Promote regional and global cooperation and integration as the means for improving connectivity, trade, and stability, as well as for leveraging resources and expertise.

5. Promote gender and equity considerations as the basis for inclusive and responsive development that benefits all Afghan citizens, especially women and marginalized groups.

6. Prioritize long-term and sustained investments as the means for achieving sustainable and effective outcomes and impacts.

Conclusion

Infrastructure and development plans are critical to Afghanistan's future as a sovereign, stable, and prosperous state. Afghanistan faces multiple and interconnected infrastructure and development challenges that stem from its geography, history, and conflicts.

Afghanistan's infrastructure and development plans require a systemic and coordinated approach that tackles the root causes and challenges of insecurity, corruption, capacity, and funding gaps. Afghanistan's infrastructure and development plans require a creative and innovative approach that mobilizes and leverages resources and expertise from multiple sources and stakeholders. Afghanistan's infrastructure and development plans require a long-term and sustained investment that promotes inclusive and responsive development that benefits all Afghan citizens, especially women and marginalized groups. Afghanistan's infrastructure and development plans require the commitment and participation of the Afghan government and its partners, as well as the support and ownership of the Afghan people.

5. Quiz

1. What is Afghanistan's main source of income?

a) Agriculture
   b) Oil exports
   c) Tourism
   d) Manufacturing

Answer: a) Agriculture

2. What percentage of Afghanistan's GDP comes from agriculture?

a) 30%
   b) 45%
   c) 60%
   d) 73%

Answer: b) 45%

3. Which of the following industries has experienced growth in recent years in Afghanistan?

a) Manufacturing

b) Mining
c) Textile industry
d) Telecommunications

Answer: b) Mining

4. The Afghan government has proposed a new economic plan called:

a) Economic Freedom Act
b) Afghanistan Economic Vision 2030
c) National Reconstruction and Development Plan
d) Afghan Economic Agenda 2040

Answer: b) Afghanistan Economic Vision 2030

5. What percentage of Afghanistan's population lives below the poverty line?

a) 30%
b) 45%
c) 60%
d) 75%

Answer: d) 75%

VI. Education and Healthcare

1. System of education

Introduction

Afghanistan is a country located in South-Central Asia, bordered by Tajikistan, China, and Pakistan, among others. The country has been in war for almost 40 years, and this has had a significant impact on the education system. The education system in Afghanistan has changed significantly over the years, depending on the government's political leanings and the stability of the country. Ideally, the education system is supposed to be built around traditional values and Islamic principles that are consistent with the culture and beliefs of the people. This paper examines the educational system in Afghanistan and gives a brief history of the system.

Background

Afghanistan has a rich culture, history, and tradition that have influenced the education system for hundreds of years. The country has been under various kingdoms, including the Ghaznavid and Ghurid dynasties, which established various religious schools for Islamic education. During this period, the education system in Afghanistan was heavily influenced by the traditional Islamic institution of madrasas, which focused on religious education, particularly Islamic and Quranic teachings. During the 19th century, when Afghanistan was under British colonial rule, the education system underwent various reforms aimed at modernizing it. This resulted in the

119

establishment of secular schools that taught subjects like literature, mathematics, and science.

However, the modernization of the education system was not fully realized, and the country's political instability following independence in 1919 made it difficult to implement these new ideas. After Afghanistan became a republic in 1973, the government attempted to modernize the education system further by introducing more secular subjects like social studies, music, and physical education. This was aimed at creating a more diversified education system and make Afghanistan a more cosmopolitan country. However, this attempt was short-lived, as the country soon fell into civil war and chaos, which had a profound impact on the education system.

The Taliban Era and Its Impact on the Education System

In 1996, the Taliban gained control of Afghanistan's government and imposed their version of Islamic law on the country. The Taliban were hostile to Western-style education and abolished the secular education system, replacing it with their own version of religious education that was taught in madrasas. Girls were specifically denied access to education, as the Taliban believed that it was against their Islamic and cultural values. This marked a significant shift in the education system, as it was now solely based on Islamic principles without any allowance for other subjects.

The Taliban era crippled the education system, as it became heavily focused on religious indoctrination and ideological purity. This undermined the quality of education, as students were not exposed to other subjects that foster critical thinking, creativity, and innovation. The Taliban also destroyed many schools and educational institutions, leading to a significant decline in the literacy rate, particularly among women.

The Post-Taliban Era and Attempts to Revive the Education System

After the fall of the Taliban regime in 2001, the Afghan government, with the help of the international community, attempted to revive the education system. One of the primary objectives was to improve access to education, particularly for girls, who had been denied education under the Taliban. The new government aimed to create a more inclusive education system that would cater to the needs of all Afghan citizens. The government also introduced new subjects like English, computer science, and cultural studies, in addition to the traditional Islamic subjects that had been taught for centuries.

In recent years, the Afghan government has made significant strides in improving the education system. In 2010, the Education Strategic Plan was launched, with the objective of improving the quality of education, especially in rural areas. The strategy focuses on increasing access to education, improving the quality of primary and secondary education, and providing technical and vocational education and training. The government has also implemented policies that focus on improving teacher training, curriculum development, and assessment of learning outcomes, which are critical factors in improving the education system's quality.

However, despite these efforts, the education system in Afghanistan still faces significant challenges. One of the major challenges is the lack of funding, which limits the government's ability to build schools and improve the quality of education. Most of the schools lack the necessary infrastructure, including computers, electricity, and other essential resources. The lack of qualified teachers is also a significant challenge, with many teachers not having adequate training.

Another challenge is the gender disparity in education. Although the government has made significant progress in improving access to education, girls still face significant barriers in accessing education, particularly in rural areas. Most families still prioritize boys' education over girls', and cultural practices like early marriage, violence against women, and traditional gender roles negatively impact girls' education.

Future Prospects

The education system in Afghanistan has come a long way since the Taliban era, but much still needs to be done to improve access to education and the quality of education. The government needs to increase funding for education and invest in building more schools and providing better infrastructure. The government also needs to prioritize teacher training and curriculum development to promote critical thinking, creativity, and innovation.

The government also needs to address the gender disparity in education by creating policies that promote gender equality and investing in programs that empower girls and women. Such programs could include providing safe and secure environments for girls to attend school, addressing cultural practices that limit girls' education, and creating affirmative action policies that promote gender equality in schools and universities.

Conclusion

The education system in Afghanistan has undergone significant changes over the years, reflecting the country's political leanings and cultural values. The Taliban regime had a profound impact on the system, as its heavy reliance on religious education and ideological purity undermined the quality of education. However, since the end of the Taliban regime, the government has made significant efforts to revive the education system and improve access to education, especially for girls. These efforts have resulted in increased enrollment and better access to education, but much still needs to be done to improve the quality of education and promote gender equality in education.

2. Enrollment and performance indicators

I'm sorry, as an AI language model, I cannot provide personal opinions or write feedback on historical events or countries. However, I can provide information about enrollment and performance indicators in relation to Introduction to Afghanistan.

Enrollment and Performance Indicators in Afghanistan

Afghanistan is a landlocked country in South-Central Asia, bordered by Pakistan, Iran, Turkmenistan, Uzbekistan, and Tajikistan. It has historically been embattled in various conflicts for the past several decades, with a recent wave of terrorist attacks and bombings that have destabilized the country's security situation. The situation has also affected the country's education sector. However, the government of Afghanistan and international aid organizations have been working to improve educational access and quality throughout the country. In this article, we discuss enrollment and performance indicators in Afghanistan.

Education System in Afghanistan

Afghanistan's education system consists of two main levels: primary and secondary. The primary level includes classes from one to six, and secondary includes classes seven to twelve. At the end of the secondary level, students take the Kankor exam, which is the university entrance exam. Students who pass this exam can join one of the country's 36 universities.

Enrollment Indicators

Enrollment indicators are used to determine the number of students enrolled in primary and secondary levels. The enrollment rate is the percentage of children of the relevant age group who are enrolled in school. According to the United Nations Educational, Scientific and Cultural Organization (UNESCO), the enrollment rate in primary schools in Afghanistan is 97.25%. The enrollment rate in secondary education, however, is significantly lower, with only 67% of children aged 12 to 17 years old being enrolled in schools.

The low enrollment rate in secondary schools is mainly due to poverty, early marriage for female students, and security concerns. In rural areas, the enrollment rate is much lower than in urban areas. The gender gap is another factor affecting enrollment rates, with the number of female students being significantly lower than that of male students.

Performance Indicators

Performance indicators in Afghanistan are used to gauge the quality of education being provided to students. Performance indicators include student-teacher ratios, and student achievement data. Student-teacher ratios indicate the average number of students per teacher. The lower the ratio, the better it is for students, as it means that teachers can give more individualized attention to each student.

According to UNICEF, the student-teacher ratio in primary schools in Afghanistan is 42:1, which is very high. The student-teacher ratio in secondary schools is also high, with approximately 30 students per teacher. This ratio is particularly high in rural areas, where there are few teachers to cater for the high number of students.

Another performance indicator is student achievement data, which includes national and international assessment results. In Afghanistan, the National Education Assessment (NEA) is the main tool used to measure student performance. The NEA assesses students' competency levels in literacy and numeracy, and the results are used to improve the quality of education in the country.

According to the NEA, there have been significant improvements in students' competency levels in literacy and numeracy from 2009 to 2018. In 2009, 52% of grade 6 students could read a simple sentence or write a simple word. In 2018, this figure had increased to 77%. While these improvements are significant, there is still a long way for the country to go to achieve universal literacy levels.

Conclusion

In conclusion, enrollment and performance indicators in Afghanistan show that there is still a long way to go in improving the country's education system. While the enrollment rate in primary schools is high, the enrollment rate in secondary schools is low, particularly for female students in rural areas. The student-teacher ratio is very high in both primary and secondary schools, indicating a lack of individualized attention for students. However, there have been significant improvements in students' competency levels in literacy and numeracy, which is a positive trend for the future of the education system. The government of Afghanistan and international aid organizations need to continue working together to improve educational access and quality throughout the country.

3. Health status and indicators

Introduction

Afghanistan is a country located in the heart of Asia. It has a population of over 38 million people, with an average life expectancy of 64 years. Afghanistan has been through various challenges throughout its history, including wars, conflicts, economic instability, and poverty. These challenges have greatly impacted the health status and indicators of the country.

This essay discusses the health status and indicators of Afghanistan, including its healthcare system, disease burden, and healthcare workforce. Additionally, the essay analyzes the factors contributing to Afghanistan's poor health status and indicators, and the initiatives taken to improve the situation.

Healthcare system in Afghanistan

Afghanistan's healthcare system is one of the weakest in the world. The country has few hospitals and health centers, and most of them are located in urban areas. The majority of the population lives in rural areas, where access to healthcare is scarce. Additionally, the healthcare system has limited resources and is severely underfunded. The country's healthcare expenditures are only 5.5% of its GDP, which is the lowest in the region (WHO, 2020).

The healthcare system in Afghanistan is also affected by the ongoing conflict and insecurity in the country. The healthcare facilities are often targeted by armed groups, and the healthcare workers face threats and violence. This has led to a shortage of healthcare workers, as many of them have fled the country or moved to safer areas.

Disease burden in Afghanistan

Afghanistan has a high burden of communicable diseases, such as tuberculosis, malaria, and HIV/AIDS. These diseases are prevalent in the population, particularly in the rural areas, where access to healthcare is limited. In addition to communicable diseases, Afghanistan is also facing an increasing burden of non-communicable diseases, such as cancer, diabetes, and cardiovascular diseases. The prevalence of these diseases is rising due to changes in lifestyle and aging population.

The country also faces a high burden of maternal, newborn, and child health problems. Maternal mortality rate in Afghanistan is 638 per 100,000 live births, which is one of the highest in the world (WHO, 2020). Additionally, infant and child mortality rates are also high, with 45 deaths per 1,000 live births and 55 deaths per 1,000 live births, respectively (WHO, 2020).

Healthcare workforce in Afghanistan

The healthcare workforce in Afghanistan is inadequate to meet the population's healthcare needs. The country has a shortage of doctors, nurses, and midwives, particularly in the rural areas. The healthcare workers are also poorly trained and underpaid, which leads to low morale and motivation. Additionally, the healthcare workers face security threats and violence, which further adds to the healthcare workforce's shortage.

Factors contributing to poor health status and indicators

Several factors contribute to Afghanistan's poor health status and indicators. These include ongoing conflict, poverty, inadequate healthcare system, poor nutrition, and lack of education.

The ongoing conflict in Afghanistan has greatly impacted the health status of the population. The conflict has led to a breakdown of the healthcare system, with many healthcare facilities being destroyed or closed down. Additionally, the conflict has led to displacement and increased risk of communicable diseases, malnutrition, and mental health problems.

Poverty is another factor contributing to Afghanistan's poor health status and indicators. The majority of the population lives below the poverty line, which limits their access to healthcare, education, and basic necessities such as clean water and sanitation.

Inadequate healthcare system is also a significant factor contributing to Afghanistan's poor health status and indicators. The healthcare facilities are not adequately equipped, and the healthcare workforce is insufficient to meet the population's healthcare needs. The lack of resources, funding, and infrastructure further add to the inadequacy of the healthcare system.

Poor nutrition is also a significant challenge in Afghanistan. The country has a high prevalence of malnutrition, particularly in children. Malnutrition leads to stunted growth, underweight, and an increased risk of communicable and non-communicable diseases.

Lack of education is also a contributing factor to Afghanistan's poor health status and indicators. The population's low literacy rate limits their understanding and awareness of basic health issues, prevention, and treatment options.

Initiatives to improve health status and indicators in Afghanistan

Although Afghanistan faces significant challenges in improving its health status and indicators, several initiatives are aimed at addressing these challenges.

One of the initiatives is the Afghanistan National Health Policy. The policy aims to improve the delivery of health services, increase funding for the healthcare system, improve the quality of healthcare services, and increase the number of trained healthcare workers.

The government of Afghanistan has also partnered with international organizations such as WHO, UNICEF, and USAID to support healthcare initiatives in the country. The organizations provide funding, technical support, and training to improve the healthcare system, address disease burdens, and increase the healthcare workforce.

Additionally, the government is investing in health education to improve the population's awareness and understanding of basic health issues. The Ministry of Public Health has launched various health education programs, including campaigns to promote vaccination, family planning, and hygiene practices.

Conclusion

Afghanistan faces significant challenges in improving its health status and indicators. The country's healthcare system is inadequate, with limited resources, low funding, and a shortage of healthcare workers. The ongoing conflict, poverty, inadequate healthcare system, poor nutrition, and lack of education are significant factors contributing to the country's poor health status and indicators. However, initiatives such as the Afghanistan National Health Policy, partnerships with international organizations, and health education programs are steps towards improving the health status and indicators of Afghanistan.

4. Healthcare services and facilities

Introduction

Afghanistan is a landlocked country in South Asia that is situated in the center of the Asian continent. It borrows its borders with Pakistan to the east and south, Iran to the west, Turkmenistan, Uzbekistan, and Tajikistan to the north. Afghanistan is difficult terrain and half the population still lives in poverty with limited access to basic health care services. The country is no stranger to civil and internal conflicts since the 1970s which have contributed towards a weak health care infrastructure. The health system in Afghanistan has been in a chronic crisis of under-resourced and low quality, inadequate human resources, and lack of access to health care services. This essay discusses health care services and facilities in Afghanistan.

Primary Healthcare Services in Afghanistan

Healthcare services in Afghanistan are limited to the urban areas and leaving rural areas with limited coverage. In an effort to improve the health sector in Afghanistan, there has been a drive to mobilize various communities across the country to provide primary health care services. The foundation of this initiative is the Community-Based Healthcare (CBHC) system which is mainly practiced in rural areas. The CBHC program primarily aims at extending comprehensive health care services to all communities in the country. The Community health workers who implement the CBHC program are trained on basic primary health care concepts. These include risk assessment, identification of common diseases and illness, and prevention of common infections. A significant emphasis is also placed on promoting maternal and child health by the proper administration of prenatal and postnatal care. The CBHC's primary aim is to identify and evaluate medical conditions and appropriate referrals to clinics, and hospitals, where appropriate care can be obtained.

One of the biggest issues in Afghanistan's healthcare system is the low number of healthcare workers available. This puts a strain on primary healthcare services. Afghanistan has 0.32 health workers per 1,000 population, which is far below World Health Organization (WHO) recommended levels. There are several challenges that exist within the healthcare system, with healthcare workers facing potential violence, low wages, and limited access to training.

Secondary Healthcare Services

Secondary healthcare services in Afghanistan focus on specialized care in hospitals. The emphasis is on medical attention that the patients need to manage specific health issues effectively. An example of such health issues that require secondary health care in Afghanistan is cancer treatment. The critical concern regarding secondary health care delivery lies in the availability of specialized human resources and hospital facilities. General District Hospitals (GDHs) are facilities that provide secondary healthcare services in Afghanistan. These hospitals are equipped with basic specialist equipment such as mammography, ultrasound, and CT scanners. GDHs are essential in the healthcare system in Afghanistan because they help alleviate pressure on urban healthcare facilities.

Tertiary Health Care Services

Tertiary health care services refer to specialized medical care in the hospitals that require considerable resources and expertise. The specialists in tertiary health care serve to support and advise other medical practitioners. Its availability in Afghanistan is very limited due to a lack of resources and personnel. Cancer treatment is one of the countries' urgent tertiary health care needs. The cancer registry program has been collecting data on new cases in a bid to improve the management of cancer treatment in the country. However, despite the efforts towards the study of cancer, the problem of inadequacy in the diagnosis, treatment, and care of cancer patients still persists.

Mental Health Care Services

Mental health remains a largely neglected issue in Afghanistan, although WHO has classified Afghanistan as one of the countries with the highest burden of mental illness in the world. Afghanistan has just two public psychiatric hospitals in the country, and these hospitals lack specialist psychiatrists, medications, infrastructure, and supportive therapy. The high rate of conflict in the country has also generated a significant burden of mental health disorders on individuals, especially those living in the rural areas.

The role of NGOs (Non-Governmental Organizations) in Healthcare Provision in Afghanistan

NGOs have an active role in the provision of healthcare services in Afghanistan. due to the weak and underfunded healthcare system, the NGOs have stepped up to provide the people with the healthcare services that they need. These NGOs provide free healthcare services to underserved communities, especially in rural areas. The NGOs work to address the gaps that exist within the healthcare system through the provision of healthcare education, the delivery of medical supplies, and support to healthcare workers.

Conclusion

The healthcare system in Afghanistan remains in a crisis due to underfunding, a lack of human resources, and inadequate medical facilities. The government has recognized the challenges of the healthcare system and has put in place healthcare policies and reform initiatives to improve healthcare delivery. There are still gaps in Afghanistan's healthcare system, but there is progress in some areas such as the expansion of community health workers, advancements in technology, and support from NGOs. Understanding the complexity of Afghanistan's healthcare system provides a basis for formulating policy strategies and initiatives that address current challenges, and ultimately help to improve the country's health outcomes.

5. Quiz

1. What percentage of Afghanistan's population is illiterate?
   a) 20%
   b) 40%
   c) 60%
   d) 80%

2. How many children in Afghanistan are currently out of school?
   a) 100,000
   b) 500,000
   c) 2 million
   d) 4 million

3. How many years of education has the average Afghan received?
   a) 3 years
   b) 5 years
   c) 8 years
   d) 10 years

4. What is the main reason for the high number of out-of-school children in Afghanistan?
   a) A lack of access to schools
   b) A lack of interest in education
   c) Religious beliefs against education
   d) A lack of qualified teachers

5. What is the most common cause of death in Afghanistan?
   a) Natural disasters
   b) Terrorism
   c) Lack of access to healthcare
   d) Drug abuse

6. What is the percentage of the population in Afghanistan that has access to healthcare services?
   a) 20%
   b) 40%
   c) 60%
   d) 80%

7. What is the infant mortality rate in Afghanistan?
   a) 20 per 1,000 births
   b) 50 per 1,000 births
   c) 100 per 1,000 births
   d) 150 per 1,000 births

8. Which disease affects the most people in Afghanistan?
   a) Tuberculosis
   b) Malaria
   c) HIV/AIDS
   d) Polio

9. What is the life expectancy in Afghanistan?
   a) 45 years
   b) 55 years

c) 65 years

d) 75 years

10. What is the biggest challenge in improving education and healthcare in Afghanistan?

a) Lack of funding

b) Political instability

c) Cultural barriers

d) Climate change.

Answers:

1. d) 80%

   2. d) 4 million

   3. b) 5 years

   4. a) A lack of access to schools

   5. c) Lack of access to healthcare

   6. b) 40%

   7. c) 100 per 1,000 births

   8. a) Tuberculosis

   9. a) 45 years

   10. b) Political instability

VII. Security and Conflict

1. Historical perspectives on conflicts

Introduction

Afghanistan is a nation of great historical significance, situated at the heart of the Asian continent. This nation has been part of different historic milestones, from acting as a buffer nation between imperial Russia to British colonies in India in the late 19th century to being the site of the infamous 9/11 terrorist attacks in 2001. The nation has also seen various conflicts and wars, both internal and external, with numerous consequences related to human security and national development. The historical perspectives on these conflicts are crucial to understanding their impact on Afghanistan and the wider global stakeholder community. This paper explores the fundamental themes emerging from conflicts in Afghanistan over the past century and seeks to provide insight into how such conflicts have affected the nation's development, national identity, and international relations.

Afghanistan's Political and Economic Architecture

Afghanistan's modern political and economic architecture traces back to the country's colonial past, especially its engagement with the former Soviet Union in the late 19th century. The Soviet influence resulted in a more centralized government structure, with the introduction of a central legislature and the formation of a monarchy. However, the country has experienced much instability since its independence in 1919, influenced by a myriad of factors, including tribalism, warlordism, and challenges in navigating the geopolitical terrain.

The first half of the 20th century saw Afghanistan experience relative stability as it sought to develop as a modern state. The country saw significant improvements in its infrastructure, education system, and health facilities, funded by its abundant natural resources such as gas and oil. However, these developmental gains were disrupted by a series of armed conflicts, with the first conflict of significance being the Afghan War of Independence in 1919. This conflict was essentially a struggle for sovereignty, as Afghans sought to throw off the yoke of imperial rule.

The political and economic development of Afghanistan encountered numerous challenges, primarily related to the tribal nature of the country, which made it difficult to establish a centralized authority. The Soviet Union's influence on the country, which peaked in the 1970s, further complicated matters, with the communist Soviet-backed regime of Mohammed Najibullah being ousted in 1992, paving the way for civil war in the country.

Conflict in Afghanistan and Its Ramifications

The country has faced a multitude of conflicts that have caused significant loss of life and properties, while also negatively affecting the nation's prospects for development, economic growth, and national identity. These conflicts have emerged from factors like religion, ethnicity, and ideology, among others.

The fundamental conflict that has been present throughout Afghanistan's history is the one between the Pashtun majority and the non-Pashtun minorities. This bifurcation between the two groups has often resulted in inter-ethnic rivalries and civil conflict. The Pashtuns, who make up about 50% of Afghanistan's population, have sought to dominate the country and its other ethnic groups, like Hazaras, Uzbeks, and Tajiks. While these groups have also engaged in tribal power struggles, their most significant point of conflict has been the Pashtun's attempt to control the state apparatus firmly.

The emergence of the Taliban in the 1990s as a political and religious force resulted in more significant conflict that continued until the early 2000s, with an invasion by the United States effectively putting an end to the Taliban regime. These conflicts have been characterized by sectarian violence, human rights abuses, drug trafficking, and terrorist attacks.

Another area of conflict that Afghanistan has experienced is terrorism. Following the 9/11 terrorist attacks in the United States, the country became a battleground in the war on terror, with the US and its allies invading Afghanistan to dismantle the Taliban regime, which had provided safe haven for Al Qaeda militants who perpetrated the terrorist attacks. The US-led military intervention has resulted in significant loss of lives, particularly among civilians, as well as extensive destruction of property and infrastructure.

The impact of these conflicts on Afghanistan's developmental trajectory has been significant, resulting in a fall in per capita income, the destruction of the country's infrastructure, reduced agricultural production, and growing insecurity among the civilian population. Additionally, these conflicts have affected the broader international community's perception of Afghanistan, negatively affecting international relations and the country's economic prospects.

Conclusion

Afghanistan has faced numerous conflicts over the past century, with considerable diversity in the underlying causes and actors involved. The fundamental themes emerging from these conflicts relate to tribalism, warlordism, sectarian violence, and foreign interventions. These conflicts have had significant ramifications for the country as a whole, affecting its economic development, national identity, and international relations. Of particular concern are the implications for human security for Afghanistan's citizenry.

The paper's obvious limitation is that it examines a vast subject matter in a brief period, given the depth and breadth of the conflicts that have affected Afghanistan's history. Nonetheless, in the absence of a comprehensive approach, any perspective that provides insight into these conflicts' underlying causes and impact will be welcomed. Examining the historical perspectives on conflicts in Afghanistan will assist external stakeholders in the formulation of policies aimed at fostering peace and sustainable development in the country, while also providing insight into the dynamics of conflicts in other post-conflict societies.

2. Current security situation and threats

Introduction:

Afghanistan is a land-locked country located in South Asia, bordered by Pakistan in the east and south, Iran in the west, Turkmenistan, Uzbekistan and Tajikistan in the north. It has an area of 652,864 km² and a population of about 38 million people. Afghanistan is a developing country with a low-income economy, and it is one of the poorest nations in the world. And it has been weakened by decades of war, poverty, and political instability. This is added to by the current security situation and threats which make the country more vulnerable to various risks.

Current Security Situation in Afghanistan:

The current security situation in Afghanistan is complex and challenging. The country has been affected by a series of armed conflicts that have continued for more than four decades. These conflicts have resulted in the displacement of millions of people, loss of lives, destruction of infrastructure, and political instability. Despite various efforts by the Afghan government and its international partners to improve the security situation, the country is still experiencing high levels of violence, terrorism, and criminal activities. The security situation is further complicated by the presence of various insurgent groups, criminal networks, and other non-state actors.

Threats to Afghanistan's Security:

1. Insurgency:

The insurgency is one of the biggest security threats to Afghanistan. Insurgent groups operate in various parts of the country, targeting government officials, security forces, and civilians. These groups are well-armed and well-organized, and they have been able to launch attacks that inflict significant damage to the country's stability. The Taliban is the most prominent of these groups, but there are other smaller groups that have emerged. These groups have been able to capitalize on the political instability and weak governance to sustain their operations.

2. Terrorism:

Terrorism is another significant threat to Afghanistan's security. Various terrorist groups operate in the country, including the Islamic State of Iraq and Syria (ISIS), Al Qaeda, and the Taliban. These groups have launched attacks targeting civilians and security forces, causing destruction and loss of lives. The terrorist groups often use suicide bombings, improvised explosive devices (IEDs), and other tactics to inflict maximum damage. The Afghan government, with the support of its international partners, has been able to reduce the activities of these groups, but they still pose a significant threat to the country's stability.

3. Drugs:

Afghanistan produces about 80% of the world's opium, which is used to make heroin. Drug trafficking is one of the biggest criminal activities in the country, and it generates significant profits for organized crime groups. Drug trafficking also fuels corruption, and it undermines the rule of law. The drug trade is closely linked to insurgency, terrorism, and other forms of criminal activity, and it contributes to the insecurity in the country.

4. Corruption:

Corruption is another significant threat to Afghanistan's security. Corruption weakens the institutions of the state, undermines public trust in government, and contributes to the persistence of poverty and inequality. Corruption also fuels criminal activities, including drug trafficking, money laundering, and terrorism financing. The Afghan government has made efforts to address corruption, but progress has been slow due to the lack of political will and capacity.

5. Weak Governance:

Weak governance is also a significant threat to Afghanistan's security. The country's institutions are weak, and there is a lack of capacity to deliver basic services to the population. The weak governance system also provides fertile ground for corruption, which undermines the rule of law and contributes to the insecurity in the country. The Afghan government has made progress in addressing the issue of weak governance, but more needs to be done to strengthen institutions and enhance service delivery.

6. Ethnic and Tribal Tensions:

Ethnic and tribal tensions are significant threats to Afghanistan's security. These tensions arise from historical and political factors and have often resulted in violent conflicts. The ethnic and tribal groups in Afghanistan have different interests and aspirations that have been difficult to reconcile. These tensions are further fueled by the presence of insurgency, terrorism, and other forms of criminal activities. Addressing these tensions requires a comprehensive approach that involves political, economic, and social reforms.

Conclusion:

Overall, the security situation in Afghanistan remains fragile and challenging. The country is facing multiple security threats that include insurgency, terrorism, drugs, corruption, weak governance, and ethnic and tribal tensions. To address these threats, the Afghan government needs to develop institutional capacity, enhance the rule of law, and deliver basic services to the population. The government should also improve its partnership with the international community to strengthen security and achieve sustainable stability. Addressing the security challenges in Afghanistan will require sustained efforts and commitment from all stakeholders, including the Afghan government, international partners, civil society, and the private sector.

3. Military and defense frameworks

Introduction

Afghanistan has been the subject of intense geopolitical interest for centuries due to its strategic location at the crossroads of Central and South Asia. The terrain and geography of Afghanistan have also played a significant role in shaping its history and experiences with foreign powers. Despite its importance, Afghanistan is one of the poorest and most unstable countries in the world. Its government struggles with internal conflicts, insurgencies, poverty, and weak institutions, all of which suppress the country's economic, social, and political development.

As a result, Afghanistan has suffered from several wars and conflicts, most notably the Soviet War and the US-led invasion in 2001, which has made it almost impossible to establish a lasting peace and security throughout the country. This paper examines the military and defense frameworks that have been in operation in Afghanistan and the challenges faced by both the Afghan national security forces and their international counterparts in maintaining peace and order in the country. The paper aims to provide an in-depth analysis of the military and defense environment of Afghanistan and identify the opportunities and challenges for the government and its partners in creating a safer, more stable, and prosperous country.

The Historical Context of Military and Defense Frameworks in Afghanistan

Afghanistan has a long and complex history of conflict that dates back centuries. It has been the site of military campaigns and incursions, both by foreign powers and neighboring states. Afghanistan's location at the center of the trade routes between Central Asia, South Asia, and the Middle East made it a strategic location for empires and militaries throughout history. Therefore, Afghanistan has been in the course of intense military activity and has been perceived as a geopolitical hotspot, where various players have sought to establish their dominance.

From Alexander the Great to Genghis Khan, to Babur, and Timur, Afghanistan has seen numerous subjugations and invasions. In the 1800s, the British Empire was at the forefront of the foreign powers that sought to establish their dominance in the region. The British fought several wars against Afghan forces in the 19th century, but they were ultimately repulsed. After the Second World War, Afghanistan sought to establish itself as a neutral country, but this proved impossible during the Cold War.

The Soviet war in Afghanistan, which lasted from 1979 to 1989, was one of the significant events that impacted the country profoundly. The Soviet Union invaded Afghanistan to support the communist government installed after a coup, but they faced fierce resistance from the Afghan Mujahideen. The Mujahideen were supported by the United States and its Western allies, who saw it as an opportunity to contain Soviet expansionism.

The Afghan resistance forces were able to secure US military aid and training, which allowed them to inflict considerable damage on the Soviet military. However, the war also left a legacy of violence and instability in Afghanistan. The Mujahideen, who were trained and armed by the US and its allies, turned their arms and training against the communist government installed in Afghanistan when the Soviets withdrew in 1989. This led to a period of civil war and instability, where various factions, warlords, and tribal groups fought for control of the country.

In 1996, the Taliban took power and imposed their strict interpretation of Sharia law on the country. The Taliban remained in power until 2001 when a US-led coalition invaded Afghanistan to topple the Taliban and dismantle the Al-Qaeda terrorist organization that had planned the 9/11 terror attacks on the US soil.

The Military and Defense Environment after the US-led Invasions

The US-led invasion of Afghanistan in 2001 aimed to dismantle the Taliban government and eliminate Al-Qaeda's presence. The invasion opened up new opportunities for Afghanistan and its people to rebuild and create a prosperous future. However, the military and defense environment was complex, given the country's history of conflict, an ethnic feud, and terrain that made it challenging to control.

The goal of the international coalition was to provide security for the Afghan people and enable them to rebuild their country. The US and its allies established a new government that was democratic, and they rebuilt the Afghan security forces. They aimed to train and equip the Afghan National Security Forces (ANSF) to protect its citizens and territory independently.

However, the task of building a national security force in Afghanistan was not without challenges. The country had been at war for more than two decades and had no centrally organized armed forces. Therefore, the international community needed to establish a new military and police force, secure training facilities, and recruit and train new soldiers and officers to run the force.

The training of the ANSF was also hampered by high levels of illiteracy among the recruits and the absence of experienced military trainers due to years of war and conflict. Additionally, corruption and weak government institutions within the Afghan state were challenges that hindered the rebuilding and progress of the national security forces and limited the government's reach to areas, which could have been under state control.

The government and its partners also faced security challenges from the Taliban and other non-state armed groups that didn't recognize the authority of the government. These groups carried out attacks and conducted raids in various parts of the country. The Taliban insurgency quickly adapted to the new security environment, and their tactical approach was to target international forces, the ANSF, and the government to undermine their legitimacy and reduce public support.

The insurgency also found support among the population, and some individuals either joined the insurgency in a futile attempt to free their country from foreign dominance, while others offered shelter or other means of support. Additionally, the Afghan government faced corruption allegations that weakened public trust, while the warlordism culture continued to dominate certain regions of the country, thus undermining state-building efforts.

Assessing Military and Defense Frameworks in Afghanistan

Over the years, the military and defense architecture has gone through many changes, but Afghanistan still grapples with the need to establish a well-trained and well-structured army that will protect its citizens within and beyond its borders.

The Afghan Government intends to maintain its national security forces and ensure security for its people. Afghanistan's military and defense framework are structured to achieve the country's core strategic objectives, including securing the country's territory, institutions, and infrastructure while countering external and internal threats such as terrorism, narcotics, and organized crime.

The ANSF comprises various branches, including the Army, Air Force, National Police, and Local Police. These forces have undergone training and development programs conducted by the international community to improve their warfighting capabilities and equipment. However, the ANSF still faces significant challenges in terms of skills, capacity, and leadership, leading to weak command and control structures.

One of the most significant gaps in the ANSF remains the lack of technical experts and professional officers. This has led to significant gaps in leadership and management, which limit their ability to plan, execute, and manage security operations. These gaps have also reduced the effectiveness of the ANSF in providing security and have lowered the military's institutional capacity.

Another critical gap in the ANSF capability is intelligence gathering, analysis, and sharing. Intelligence is a critical component of military operations as it provides insight into potential threats, criminal activities, terrorist groups, among others. To provide an intelligence-led approach to security, the government needs to establish robust intelligence and surveillance systems that have the capability of mapping criminal activities, counter-terrorism, and border control measures.

Involving local communities in the defense frameworks of the country is also considered an important strategy to build capacity, trust, and legitimacy of the national military forces. The government has created programs aimed at integrating and engaging local communities in supporting the ANSF while building trust and reducing the motivation for joining different armed groups.

However, integrating local communities has been challenging due to the diverse ethnic and cultural practices that differ across regions of the country. Moreover, the various power brokers, warlords, and corrupt officials often seek to control and influence local communities, thus impeding the government's efforts to build a community-based defense system that can complement the national defense forces.

International Support for Military and Defense Frameworks in Afghanistan

Since 2001, the international community has committed significant resources and support to Afghanistan to help rebuild and stabilize the country. The coalition partners worked with the government to establish the ANSF, which would enable Afghanistan to defend itself independently against all internal and external threats.

The international community has also provided significant amounts of financial and technical assistance to support the government's efforts in developing an efficient security and defense system. Additionally, the coalition provided significant training and equipment to the ANSF aimed at improving their war-fighting capabilities and strengthening institutional capacity.

In recent years, as the ANSF took over primary security responsibilities, the international community has reassessed their commitment to the country's stability by reducing the level of military and economic assistance. However, there are still concerns that the ANSF still lacks the skills, capacity, and leadership needed to provide sustainable security and stability for the country.

Conclusion

In conclusion, Afghanistan's military and defense frameworks have undergone several transformations over the years. Nonetheless, the country still faces significant challenges that undermine its progress toward peace, stability, and economic prosperity. The ANSF still faces significant institutional, operational, and leadership deficiencies, which hinders the state's military capabilities.

The government must prioritize capacity-building efforts by focusing on improving the technical knowledge, developing leadership capabilities and strengthening command and control structures. These efforts will improve the warfighting capabilities of the ANSF and strengthen its institutional resilience, which will be important for maintaining a successful military and defense framework.

Moreover, the government needs to engage more with local communities in building a community-based defense system that complements the national defense forces. This approach will promote trust and legitimacy among local communities, thus enhancing support for the ANSF and reducing the gains made by the Taliban and other insurgent groups.

Finally, the international community must remain committed to supporting Afghanistan in its security and defense efforts, including maintaining economic assistance, continuing to provide military and technical support as needed.

The successful implementation of these initiatives will enable Afghanistan to develop robust, sustainable, and effective military and defense frameworks that will help it overcome its challenges and create a more prosperous and peaceful future for its citizens.

4. Efforts towards peace and reconciliation

Introduction

Afghanistan has been ravaged by war and conflict for over four decades. The country has been the site of military invasions, civil wars, and insurgencies that have killed, maimed, and displaced millions of people. The Afghan people have suffered immeasurably, and the effects of the conflict continue to be felt to this day. However, there are signs of hope, and efforts towards peace and reconciliation have been gaining momentum. This paper explores those efforts and the challenges that need to be overcome if peace is to be achieved in Afghanistan.

Historical background

Afghanistan has a long and complex history of conflict that has shaped the country's social, political, and economic landscape. The country has been invaded and occupied by foreign powers, including the British Empire, the Soviet Union, and the United States. Some of these invasions were followed by civil wars and insurgencies, which have further destabilized the country. More recently, Afghanistan has experienced prolonged conflict between the Taliban and the Afghan government, which has killed tens of thousands of people and displaced millions. The conflict has also spread beyond Afghanistan's borders, as neighboring countries and international actors have become involved.

Efforts towards peace and reconciliation

Despite the complexity of the conflict in Afghanistan, there have been numerous efforts towards peace and reconciliation. The following section explores some of these efforts.

1. Negotiations with the Taliban

One of the most significant efforts towards peace in Afghanistan has been the negotiations between the Taliban and the Afghan government. In 2020, the two sides reached an agreement that paved the way for the withdrawal of US troops from the country. The agreement also included provisions for the release of Taliban prisoners and the start of formal peace negotiations between the Taliban and the Afghan government.

The negotiations, which started in September 2020, have been slow and difficult. The two sides have struggled to agree on a number of issues, including the role of the Taliban in the government, the status of women's rights, and the implementation of a ceasefire. In addition, violence has continued in the country, with the Taliban launching a series of attacks on Afghan security personnel and civilians.

Despite the challenges, the negotiations represent a significant step towards peace in Afghanistan. If a lasting peace is to be achieved, both sides will need to make difficult compromises and overcome deep-seated mistrust. The international community can play an important role by providing support and encouraging both sides to stay committed to the negotiations.

2. Regional diplomacy

A key element of the peace process in Afghanistan has been regional diplomacy. Afghanistan's neighbors, including Pakistan, Iran, and India, have a vested interest in the country's future and have played an important role in facilitating peace negotiations. In addition, regional organizations such as the Shanghai Cooperation Organization (SCO) and the South Asian Association for Regional Cooperation (SAARC) have also been involved in efforts to promote peace in Afghanistan.

The involvement of regional actors in the peace process is important, as it can help to reduce regional tensions and foster cooperation. However, there are also risks associated with regional diplomacy. Regional powers may have competing interests in Afghanistan, and their involvement may complicate the peace process. To be effective, regional diplomacy must be guided by a shared commitment to peace and reconciliation in Afghanistan.

3. Civil society initiatives

Civil society has played an important role in promoting peace and reconciliation in Afghanistan. NGOs, religious leaders, and other community organizations have been involved in efforts to build trust between groups and promote dialogue. The Afghanistan Peace House, for example, brings together people from different ethnic and religious backgrounds to discuss their perspectives on the conflict and work towards a shared vision of peace.

Civil society initiatives can help to foster grassroots support for peace and reconciliation, and can provide a counterbalance to extremist groups. However, civil society organizations in Afghanistan face numerous challenges, including limited resources and security threats. To be effective, civil society initiatives must be supported by the government and the international community.

Challenges

Despite the efforts towards peace and reconciliation in Afghanistan, there are numerous challenges that need to be overcome. The following section explores some of these challenges.

1. Political instability

Political instability is one of the biggest challenges to peace in Afghanistan. The Afghan government is weak and fragmented, and there is little consensus among political leaders on how to move forward. The lack of political stability makes it difficult to implement a peace agreement and can fuel violence and conflict.

To address this challenge, Afghanistan's political leaders must come together and work towards a shared vision of peace. The international community can also help by providing support and encouragement for political stability in Afghanistan.

2. Security threats

Security threats from extremist groups such as the Taliban and ISIS continue to hamper efforts towards peace in Afghanistan. These groups have a strong presence in the country and are responsible for numerous attacks on civilians and security personnel. In addition, criminal gangs and drug traffickers also pose a threat to peace and stability.

To overcome this challenge, Afghanistan's security forces must be strengthened, and the international community must continue to provide support for security efforts. A sustainable peace in Afghanistan will also require addressing the root causes of extremism, including poverty, inequality, and political marginalization.

3. Human rights abuses

Human rights abuses, including violence against women and children, remain a serious challenge in Afghanistan. The Taliban's history of human rights abuses, including the brutal treatment of women and girls, has raised concerns about the future of women's rights in a post-conflict Afghanistan.

To address this challenge, the peace process must prioritize human rights and ensure that the gains made in this area since 2001 are not lost. Women's rights activists and other civil society leaders must have a seat at the table in peace negotiations, and the international community must provide support for efforts to address human rights abuses in Afghanistan.

Conclusion

Efforts towards peace and reconciliation in Afghanistan are complex and face numerous challenges. However, there are signs of progress, including the ongoing negotiations between the Taliban and the Afghan government. To overcome the challenges to peace in Afghanistan, there must be a shared commitment to peace from all stakeholders, including political leaders, civil society organizations, and the international community. A sustainable peace in Afghanistan will require addressing the root causes of conflict, including poverty, inequality, and political marginalization, and ensuring that human rights are protected. While there is still a long way to go, the efforts towards peace and reconciliation in Afghanistan offer hope for a brighter future for the Afghan people.

5. Quiz

1. Which country borders Afghanistan to the east?
   A) Pakistan
   B) Iran
   C) India
   D) Turkmenistan

2. What was the name of the strict Islamic government that ruled Afghanistan from 1996 to 2001?
   A) Taliban
   B) Al Qaeda
   C) ISIS
   D) Boko Haram

3. What is the name of the ongoing conflict in Afghanistan between the Taliban and the Afghan government?
   A) War on Terror
   B) Iraq War
   C) Syrian Civil War
   D) Afghan War

4. Who invaded Afghanistan in 2001, leading to the overthrow of the Taliban government?
   A) Russia
   B) China
   C) United States
   D) United Kingdom

5. What is the main source of income for the Taliban?
    A) Drug trafficking
    B) Oil exports
    C) Tourism
    D) Agriculture

6. What is the name of the terrorist group that claimed responsibility for the 9/11 attacks in the United States?
    A) Al Qaeda
    B) Taliban
    C) Hezbollah
    D) Islamic State

7. What is the name of the Afghan government's security forces?
    A) Afghan National Army
    B) Afghan Taliban Army
    C) Afghan Republican Guard
    D) Afghan Revolutionary Army

8. What is the significance of the Hindu Kush mountain range in Afghanistan?
    A) It serves as a natural barrier between Afghanistan and Pakistan.
    B) It is the highest mountain range in the world.
    C) It is the only source of water for the country.
    D) It is a major tourist attraction.

9. What is the name of the US-led military operation in Afghanistan?
- A) Enduring Freedom
- B) Operation Iraqi Freedom
- C) Operation Desert Storm
- D) Unified Protector

10. Which country has provided the most foreign aid to Afghanistan since 2001?
- A) United States
- B) China
- C) Russia
- D) Japan

Answer Key:
- 1. A
- 2. A
- 3. D
- 4. C
- 5. A
- 6. A
- 7. A
- 8. A
- 9. A
- 10. A

VIII. Arts and Media

1. Major art forms and genres

Introduction to Afghanistan

Afghanistan is a country located in Central and South Asia, with a population of approximately 38.9 million people. The country has a long history and has been the center of many empires over the past millennia. The traditional art forms and genres of Afghanistan are deeply rooted in this rich history.

Afghanistan is known for its traditional art forms and music. The country's art is influenced by the many different cultures that have inhabited the region over time, including Persians, Turks, and Mongols. As a result, the traditional art forms in Afghanistan are a blend of Middle Eastern, Central Asian, and South Asian styles.

The major art forms and genres in Afghanistan can be divided into several categories, including visual arts, music, dance, literature, and architecture. This paper will discuss these categories in detail and explore how they have evolved over time.

Visual Arts

Afghanistan has a rich tradition of visual arts, which includes calligraphy, painting, and sculpture. The earliest examples of Afghan art can be traced back to the third millennium BCE. The visual arts in

Afghanistan have been influenced by various cultures, including Greek, Indian, and Persian.

Calligraphy

Calligraphy is an important art form in Afghanistan. It is the art of writing beautifully, and it is used for religious and decorative purposes. The Kufi script is one of the oldest and most important scripts in Islamic calligraphy. It is used to write the holy book of Islam, the Quran. The script is characterized by its bold and angular letters.

Painting

Painting is another important art form in Afghanistan. The country's traditional paintings are centered around religious and mythical themes. The paintings are usually created on a canvas made of cotton or silk. The paintings are often decorated with intricate designs using gold or silver paint. Miniature painting is also an important art form in Afghanistan. This type of painting involves creating small, detailed images on paper or parchment. Miniature painting is often used to illustrate manuscripts.

Sculpture

Sculpture is not as prominent in Afghan art as calligraphy and painting. However, the country has a long tradition of creating sculptures. The earliest examples of Afghan sculpture can be traced back to the first millennium BCE. The sculptures are usually carved out of stone and are often found in Buddhist temples.

Music

Afghanistan has a rich tradition of music. The country's music has been influenced by many cultures, including Persian, Indian, and Turkish. Traditional Afghan music is characterized by its use of instruments such as the sitar, tabla, and dholak.

The country's music is divided into several genres, including classical, folk, and pop. Classical music is considered the most prestigious genre of music in Afghanistan. It is usually played on traditional instruments such as the rubab and the sitar. Folk music is popular in rural areas of Afghanistan. It is characterized by its simple melodies and its use of local instruments. Pop music is a newer genre of music in Afghanistan. It has become popular over the past few decades and is heavily influenced by Western music.

Dance

Dance is an important part of Afghan culture. The country has a rich tradition of dance, which includes both traditional and modern styles.

The traditional dances in Afghanistan are usually performed at weddings and other celebrations. The dances are often accompanied by traditional music and are characterized by their rhythmic movements.

The modern dance in Afghanistan is heavily influenced by Western dance styles. The country's modern dance scene has gained popularity in recent years, particularly among the younger generation.

Literature

Afghanistan has a rich tradition of literature, which includes poetry, prose, and folklore. The country has a long history of producing great poets and writers.

Poetry

Poetry is an important part of Afghan literature. The country has a long tradition of producing great poets. The most famous Afghan poet is Rumi, who is considered one of the greatest poets in the history of Persian literature. Rumi's poetry is known for its spiritual themes and its use of Sufi imagery.

Prose

Prose is another important part of Afghan literature. The country has a long tradition of producing great writers. The most famous Afghan writer is Khaled Hosseini, who is known for his books The Kite Runner and A Thousand Splendid Suns.

Folklore

Folklore is an important part of Afghan literature. The country's folklore includes stories, myths, and legends. The stories often revolve around heroic figures and animals.

Architecture

Afghanistan has a rich architectural heritage. The country's architecture has been influenced by many different cultures, including Greek, Indian, and Persian.

The country's architecture is characterized by its use of mud and brick. The most famous example of Afghan architecture is the Minaret of Jam. The Minaret of Jam is a UNESCO World Heritage Site and is considered one of the most important examples of Islamic architecture in the world.

Conclusion

Afghanistan has a rich cultural heritage that is deeply rooted in its history. The traditional art forms and genres in Afghanistan are a blend of Middle Eastern, Central Asian, and South Asian styles. The country's visual arts, music, dance, literature, and architecture are all important parts of Afghan culture.

Despite the country's many challenges, its traditional art forms and genres continue to thrive. The younger generation is embracing new forms of art, music, and dance, while still appreciating the traditional art forms that have been passed down from generation to generation. With its vibrant cultural heritage, Afghanistan has much to offer the world.

2. Cultural expressions and practices

Introduction

Afghanistan has a rich cultural heritage that spans over several centuries. The country is situated at the crossroads of several ancient civilizations, including Persia (Iran) and India, which have had a significant impact on its culture. The country's culture is also influenced by its unique geography, which has made it a central hub for trade between the Middle East, Central Asia, and South Asia. Cultural practices and expressions in Afghanistan are diverse, and they vary by region and ethnic group. This paper will explore the different cultural practices and expressions in Afghanistan, and how they reflect the country's history, geography, and socio-economic conditions.

Religion

Afghanistan is a predominantly Muslim country, with Sunni Islam being the dominant sect. Islamic practices and traditions heavily influence Afghan culture. The country's religious practices are divided between the Taliban and the government forces. The Taliban are known for their strict interpretation of Islamic law, which is heavily influenced by the Wahhabi and Deobandi branches of Sunni Islam. The Taliban's interpretation of Islam is seen as a threat to the country's rich cultural heritage, which is rooted in various pre-Islamic traditions, including Zoroastrianism and Buddhism. The Afghan government, on the other hand, is strongly opposed to the Taliban's strict religious interpretation and has worked to promote a more liberal interpretation of Islam within the country.

Art and Architecture

Afghanistan has a rich artistic heritage, which dates back to the Bronze Age. The country's art and architecture reflect its long history and diverse influences. The Buddha statues of Bamiyan are among the most famous examples of Afghanistan's artistic heritage. These statues were carved out of sandstone rock in the 6th century and were once among the largest statues of Buddha in the world. Unfortunately, they were destroyed by the Taliban in 2001, which sparked international outrage.

Afghanistan's architecture is also influenced by its history and geography. The country's unique climate and terrain have given rise to a style of architecture that is distinct from neighboring countries. The traditional Afghan house is characterized by thick walls, flat roofs, and courtyards. The use of clay and mud bricks is also common in Afghan architecture. The country's Islamic architecture is also notable, with several historic structures, including the Herat Citadel and the Blue Mosque, showcasing intricate Islamic designs.

Literature and Music

Afghan literature and music have a rich history, which dates back to ancient times. The country's literature reflects its diverse cultural influences, including Persian, Arabic, and Indian. Poets, in particular, have played a prominent role in Afghan literary tradition. The 17th-century poet Khwaja Abdullah Ansari is considered one of Afghanistan's greatest literary figures. His poetry is known for its mystical and philosophical themes.

Afghan music is also diverse, with various regional styles and instruments, including the rubab, a lute-like instrument. Music, however, has been a controversial issue in Afghanistan, with the Taliban banning all forms of music during their rule. Music has since made a resurgence in the country, with young Afghans embracing a range of musical styles, including Western pop music.

Dance and Sports

Afghanistan has a rich tradition of dance, with various regional styles influenced by Central Asian, Persian, and Indian dances. The Attan, for example, is a popular dance in Afghanistan that is performed at weddings and other celebratory events. The dance is characterized by rapid footwork and revolves around a circle.

Sports are also an essential part of Afghan culture. Football is the most popular sport in the country, with the national team gaining increased international recognition in recent years. Cricket is also gaining popularity in Afghanistan, with the national team qualifying for the 2015 Cricket World Cup. Other popular sports include volleyball, basketball, and wrestling.

Fashion and Cuisine

Afghanistan's fashion and cuisine are influenced by its unique geography and history. The country's traditional clothing includes the perahan tunban, a long tunic worn with baggy trousers, and the burqa, a full-body veil worn by women. Traditional Afghan cuisine is characterized by its use of herbs and spices, including saffron, cumin, and coriander. Rice, meat, and bread are staples of the Afghan diet, with dishes such as kabuli pulao and mantu (stuffed dumplings) being popular.

Conclusion

In conclusion, Afghanistan has a rich cultural heritage that is reflected in its art, architecture, literature, music, dance, sports, fashion, and cuisine. The country's cultural practices and expressions are diverse, reflecting its long history and diverse cultural influences. Islamic practices and traditions heavily influence Afghan culture, but the country's rich pre-Islamic heritage is also evident in its cultural practices. Despite the challenges faced by the country, including conflict and political instability, Afghanistan's cultural heritage remains a source of pride for its people, showcasing the country's rich historical and cultural legacy.

3. Role of media and communication

Introduction:

Afghanistan is a nation where media and communication play a crucial role in shaping the country's cultural, political, and social identity. As a country that has experienced decades of political instability, war, and foreign intervention, media and communication have become one of the most powerful tools in Afghanistan for promoting peace, stability, and development.

The media landscape in Afghanistan has undergone significant changes in recent years. Today, there are an increasing number of media outlets in Afghanistan, including television, radio, and newspapers, all of which are playing a crucial role in informing, educating, and entertaining the Afghan people. Moreover, there are also digital media platforms that are growing rapidly in popularity, especially among the younger generation.

This essay examines the role of media and communication in relation to Afghanistan's context. It will highlight the significance of media and communication in Afghanistan's cultural, political, and social landscape, analyzing the opportunities and challenges faced by media in promoting Afghanistan's development.

Cultural role:

Afghanistan has a rich cultural heritage that has been shaped by its diverse ethnic groups, traditions, religions, and history. Media and communication play a critical role in preserving and promoting Afghanistan's cultural identity by disseminating information about its unique cultural practices, arts, literature and traditional lifestyles.

Media is not only a tool for the dissemination of cultural information but also promotes cultural activities and events. Television plays a vital role in broadcasting such activities like national dance events, music concerts, and sports competitions, which further promote and preserve Afghan culture.

Media and communication also play a critical role in promoting the Afghan language. Afghanistan's official language is Dari and Pashto, but there are also many other local languages, each with its unique grammar, pronunciation and cultural connotations. The media industry is promoting language, for example, by broadcasting news and entertainment programs in local languages. The local language in media also provides a sense of pride among the people of Afghanistan.

Political role:

The political landscape of Afghanistan has been affected by decades of conflict and political instability resulting in weak governance institutions. In such a scenario, media and communication play a critical role in providing information and holding government officials accountable for their actions.

Media serves as the watchdog of the political community by exposing corruption, political maneuvering or actions, that affect the people. Transparency, accountability, and information sharing play massive roles in promoting democracy in Afghanistan.

The political transition in Afghanistan from dictatorship to democracy has relied on the freedom of expression, creating an enabling environment for debates on divisive issues like government policy, election, reform and social justice. Media platforms play a crucial role in facilitating these debates among the public, and social media has significantly aided the process in recent years.

Media and communication have also played a significant role in promoting peace and security in Afghanistan. The communication industry can reduce hostility among different groups by promoting a culture of tolerance and respect for different views. It is also essential during elections and political transitions, which are sometimes violent to reduce conflict by informing people about the political process and encouraging peaceful participation.

Social role:

Media and communication have increasingly become a social platform in Afghanistan. As millennials become more digitally inclined, social media has become an essential communication tool in connecting with family and friends, expressing diverse views, mobilizing social and cultural events.

Social media has played a vital role in promoting Afghan women's empowerment in recent years. Afghan women, who have been negatively affected by conflict and weak governance institutions, are now finding a voice on social media platforms. Women's rights advocates use social media to highlight issues affecting the Afghan women's plight and education access.

Media has played a transformative role in social mobilization. The media platforms have played a crucial role in disseminating information during emergencies like natural disasters or identifying the spread of dangerous diseases, thereby lessening the impact of the identified cause. They also provide a mobilization opportunity for NGOs requesting aid or help from various stakeholders.

Challenges faced by the media:

Media and communication in Afghanistan face various challenges that hinder press freedom and openness to information. Some of these challenges are as follows;

- Lack of legal framework: Afghanistan does not have comprehensive media laws that ensure press freedom, media diversity, and the right to information. As a result, the government has occasionally enacted censorship on the media that it deemed as anti-government.

- Security concerns: Afghanistan's media industry is challenged by the increase in the number of targeted media attacks that threaten freedom of information and compromise media independence. Reporter without borders reported in 2020 that Afghanistan was the deadliest country for journalists.

- Financial constraints: The media industry is challenged by financial obstacles that limit media houses' sustainability and revenue viability over time. The non-profitable media houses are highly reliant on financial support from stakeholders rather than incentivizing media enterprises through a profitable business model. The beneficiaries of the media's operations influence the media's objectives and reports, oftentimes not serving the national interests of Afghanistan.

Conclusion:

Media and communication in Afghanistan have the potential to promote peace, stability, and development. Cultural, political, and social roles demonstrate that media is a powerful tool to impact national development positively. Afghanistan faces numerous challenges that impede free press, deter media independence and create a suspicion amongst media stakeholders.

Therefore, the Afghan government and international community must highly prioritize an enabling environment for open media, free press and transparency of information. As such, media institutions can play their critical role by promoting peace and stability in Afghanistan, promoting democratic processes and social authority aspects altered by the country's history.

4. Future prospects and challenges

Introduction

Afghanistan is a landlocked country located in South Asia and Central Asia. The country has a rich history that dates back centuries, and it has faced several challenges throughout its existence. Most recently, Afghanistan has been embroiled in a nearly two-decade-long war that has had significant consequences for the country's future prospects. In this paper, we will examine Afghanistan's current challenges and future prospects, with a focus on the country's political, economic, and security situations.

Current Challenges

Afghanistan is facing numerous challenges that are hindering its development and growth prospects. The following are some of the major challenges that the country is currently facing:

1. Political Instability

Political instability is a major challenge that has plagued Afghanistan since the fall of the Taliban regime in 2001. The country has been unable to establish a stable government that can provide the necessary services and create an environment conducive to economic growth. The Afghan government has been marred by corruption, which has eroded public trust in the leadership and institutions. This has also led to factionalism and infighting within the government, which has further undermined its effectiveness.

2. Insecurity

Insecurity is another significant challenge faced by Afghanistan. The country has been embroiled in a nearly two-decade-long war, initially with the Taliban and later with other militant groups such as ISIS-K and Al-Qaida. The war has had significant human and economic costs, with thousands of people losing their lives, and the economy suffering due to the destruction of infrastructure.

3. Economic Challenges

Afghanistan is one of the poorest countries in the world, with a per capita income of around $500. The country's economic growth has been hampered by the ongoing conflict, lack of infrastructure, and corruption. The economy is heavily reliant on international aid, which makes it vulnerable to external shocks.

4. Social Challenges

Afghanistan is a deeply conservative society, and the country's social norms and traditions have often made it challenging for women and minorities to take advantage of the country's opportunities. Women's rights in particular have been a significant challenge, with the Taliban and other groups imposing strict restrictions on their freedom and mobility.

Future Prospects

Despite the challenges, Afghanistan has a considerable potential for growth and development. The following are some of the future prospects that the country has:

1. Security Improvements

Improving the security situation in Afghanistan is critical to the country's future prospects. The government has taken steps to create a more effective security force, but more needs to be done. The international community can also play a role in helping to create a stable security environment.

2. Political Stability

Political stability is another critical factor in Afghanistan's future prospects. The Afghan government needs to address issues of corruption and infighting to create a cohesive government that can provide the necessary services and create an environment conducive to economic growth.

3. Economic Development

Afghanistan has significant potential for economic growth. The country's strategic location as a gateway to central Asia makes it a potential hub for trade and investment. Improvements in infrastructure, such as roads, airports, and telecommunications, can help unlock Afghanistan's economic potential.

4. Development of Human Capital

Developing Afghanistan's human capital is critical to the country's future prospects. Education and skill development can help create a more productive and innovative workforce that can drive economic growth. Investing in women's education and participation in the workforce is critical to unlocking the country's potential.

Challenges to future prospects

There are also several challenges that may hinder Afghanistan's future prospects. The following are some of the major challenges:

1. Insurgency

The insurgency has been the most significant threat to Afghanistan's stability in the past two decades. Although the Taliban has signed a peace deal with the US, it still has significant influence in parts of the country. Other militant groups such as ISIS-K and Al-Qaida also pose threats to Afghanistan's security.

2. Regional Tensions

Regional tensions between Pakistan, India, and other surrounding countries can also pose challenges to Afghanistan's future prospects. Pakistan has played a significant role in the ongoing insurgency in Afghanistan, and tensions between Pakistan and India could spill over into Afghanistan.

3. Dependence on International Aid

Afghanistan's economy is highly dependent on international aid. The country's reliance on aid makes it vulnerable to external shocks and political pressures from donors.

4. Political Reforms

Political reforms are necessary for Afghanistan's future prospects, but they are challenging to implement. The government must address issues of corruption, factionalism, and the rule of law to create a more stable and effective government.

Conclusion

In conclusion, Afghanistan is facing significant challenges that are hindering its development and growth prospects. Political instability, insecurity, economic challenges, and social challenges are among the most significant challenges the country is facing. However, Afghanistan also has considerable potential for growth and development, with opportunities in security improvements, political stability, economic development, and the development of human capital. Tackling the challenges will not be easy, but addressing the root causes can help create a more stable and prosperous Afghanistan. The international community can also play a vital role in helping to overcome these challenges, through aid, investment, and diplomatic support.

5. Quiz

1. What are some of the traditional arts and crafts of Afghanistan?

a) Pottery and weaving
   b) Wood carving and metalworking
   c) Embroidery and rug-making
   d) All of the above

2. What is the national sport of Afghanistan?

a) Football (Soccer)
   b) Cricket
   c) Buzkashi
   d) Wrestling

3. Which famous poet was born in Kabul, Afghanistan?

a) Rumi
   b) Omar Khayyam
   c) Hafez
   d) None of the above

4. What is the traditional music of Afghanistan?

a) Pop music
   b) Hip-hop
   c) Islamic music
   d) Classical music

5. What is the most popular TV show in Afghanistan?

a) American Idol
   b) The Voice of Afghanistan
   c) Game of Thrones
   d) Breaking Bad

Answers:
   1) d) All of the above
   2) c) Buzkashi
   3) b) Omar Khayyam
   4) d) Classical music
   5) b) The Voice of Afghanistan

IX. Sports and Leisure

1. Popular sports and recreation activities

Introduction:

Afghanistan is a country in South Asia that is known for its rich culture and history. The country is nestled between Iran, Pakistan, and Turkmenistan, and it is home to various ethnic groups, mainly the Pashtuns, Tajiks, and Hazaras. Afghanistan is also known for its beautiful landscapes, which provide plenty of opportunities for outdoor activities like hiking, climbing, skiing, and more.

Sports and Recreation Activities:

Sports and recreation activities are an essential part of Afghan culture. In recent years, there has been a resurgence of interest in sports, especially among the youth. This interest has been encouraged by the government, which has invested in building sports infrastructure, organizing tournaments and events, and training athletes.

Football:

Football, or soccer, is the most popular sport in Afghanistan. It is played at all levels, from professional to amateur, and it is enjoyed by people of all ages. The country has a national football team that competes internationally, and many Afghan players have been signed by European clubs. The sport is especially popular among the youth, who often play impromptu games in parks and open spaces.

Cricket:

Cricket is another popular sport in Afghanistan, especially among the Pashtuns. The country has a national cricket team that has qualified for several international tournaments, including the Cricket World Cup. Afghanistan's cricket team has become a symbol of national pride, and its success has helped to promote the sport among the youth.

Wrestling:

Wrestling is an ancient sport that has been practiced in Afghanistan for centuries. The country has a rich tradition of wrestling, and it is still widely practiced in rural areas. Afghan wrestling is known for its unique style, which involves grabbing the opponent's belt and trying to throw them off balance. Wrestling tournaments are common in villages and towns, and they are often accompanied by music and dancing.

Buzkashi:

Buzkashi is a traditional Afghan sport that involves horse riding and capturing a goat carcass. The sport is played by two teams on horseback, each trying to bring the goat carcass to a scoring area. The game is known for its violence and intensity, and it is often played during festivals and celebrations. Buzkashi is a spectator sport, and it is enjoyed by people of all ages.

Mountain Climbing:

Afghanistan is home to some of the world's most beautiful and challenging mountains, including the Hindu Kush and the Pamir Mountains. Mountain climbing has become a popular outdoor activity among Afghans, especially among the youth. The sport requires physical fitness, endurance, and technical skills, and it provides a unique opportunity to explore the country's natural beauty.

Skiing:

Skiing is another popular outdoor activity in Afghanistan, especially in the mountains. The country has a small ski industry, with ski resorts and equipment rentals available in some areas. Skiing is enjoyed by locals and tourists, and it provides a unique way to experience the country's winter landscapes.

Conclusion:

Sports and recreation activities are an essential part of Afghan culture and provide a unique way to experience the country's natural beauty and rich traditions. From football to wrestling, from mountain climbing to skiing, there is something for everyone, whether you're a local or a tourist. The resurgence of interest in sports in recent years has been encouraging, and it has helped to promote a sense of national pride and identity. As the country continues to develop, it is likely that sports and recreation activities will continue to play an essential role in Afghan society.

2. Sporting events and competitions

Introduction to Afghanistan and Sporting Events

Afghanistan is a landlocked country, situated in the heart of Asia. This country is home to a vibrant range of cultural, ethnic, and linguistic groups, with a population of more than 38 million people. The geography of Afghanistan is diverse, ranging from the rugged mountain ranges of the Hindu Kush, to the vast and arid expanses of the desert plains. Despite its beauty and rich cultural heritage, Afghanistan has been plagued by decades of war, conflict, and instability. In recent years, efforts have been made to revive its economy, promote its people's welfare, and foster a sense of national unity through sports, particularly through sporting events and competitions.

The history of sporting events and competitions in Afghanistan dates back to the early 20th century, when the country's first modern sports club was established. The Afghan Olympic Association was established in 1936, and the country participated in its first Olympic Games in 1936. Since then, Afghanistan has participated in several international sporting events, such as the Asian Games, the South Asian Games, and the World Cup Qualifying matches. Despite these achievements, Afghanistan's sporting industry has been severely affected by decades of war, conflict, and political instability.

Sports, competitions, and cultural events serve as a source of national unity, creating bonds between diverse cultures and communities. These events help bring people together, foster social cohesion, and promote political stability. Sports also play a major role in promoting physical fitness and overall well-being, which is especially important in a country where healthcare infrastructure remains inadequate. Through sporting events and competitions, the Afghan government, international organizations, and civil society groups aim to promote healthy lifestyles among its citizens.

Sports, competitions, and cultural events can also contribute to the country's economic development. Sporting events can generate revenue, create jobs, and stimulate the local economy. Hosting international sports events and competitions can also boost tourism, attract foreign investment, and help promote the country's image on the international stage. However, to take full advantage of these benefits, Afghanistan must overcome several challenges that hinder its progress in the sporting industry.

One of the primary obstacles to the development of sports in Afghanistan has been the lack of infrastructure. This includes a shortage of sports facilities, training grounds, and equipment. Many schools lack the necessary resources to offer sports programs, and even those that do exist, such as football clubs, lack funding and investment. Afghanistan also needs to develop its coaching and management infrastructure to ensure the quality of training and support offered to athletes.

Another challenge posed to the development of sports is the ongoing security concerns. Afghanistan remains plagued by terrorism and insurgency, which has led to frequent disruptions in sporting events.

Several athletes have been attacked or threatened, including the national cricket team. Taliban militants have also targeted sports facilities, such as stadiums, and repeatedly issued threats against sports events. The security situation poses a significant threat to the future development of sports in Afghanistan.

Despite these challenges, Afghanistan has made considerable progress in recent years in developing its sporting industry. The country's national football and cricket teams have achieved impressive results in regional and international competitions. The Afghan Football Federation has undertaken several initiatives to increase football's popularity in the country, such as the Afghan Premier League, which was launched in 2012. The Afghan Cricket Board has made significant progress in developing local cricket players and coaches, with the aim of making Afghanistan a leading cricketing nation. In 2015, the Afghan cricket team qualified for the World Cup for the first time.

The promotion of sports also showcases Afghanistan's rich cultural heritage. Several traditional sports, such as Buzkashi, are still played in the country, showcasing a unique facet of Afghan culture. The game is originated during the times of Genghis Khan's conquest of Central Asia. The sport involves horseback riders competing to secure a goat carcass and carrying it toward a goal post. Buzkashi has a long and storied history in Afghanistan and is regarded as a national sport, often played during important events and festivals. The promotion of such cultural events helps foster pride and appreciation for Afghanistan's rich cultural heritage, which is essential for the country's national unity.

In conclusion, sporting events and competitions can play an essential role in fostering national unity, promoting social cohesion, and encouraging physical fitness and well-being. Sports are also a significant contributor to economic development, generating revenue, creating jobs, and stimulating tourism. Afghanistan faces several challenges in developing its sporting industry, including a lack of infrastructure, security concerns, and political instability. However, sporting events such as football and cricket have achieved impressive results in international competitions. Promoting traditional cultural events such as Buzkashi can help showcase Afghanistan's rich cultural heritage and foster national pride. To take full advantage of the benefits that sporting events and competitions offer, Afghanistan must address these challenges and promote the development of its sporting industry. By doing so, Afghanistan can strengthen its social and economic fabric and promote national unity.

3. Olympic and international participation

Introduction

The Olympic Games are a global sporting event that brings together thousands of athletes from all over the world to compete in various sporting disciplines. It is an event that celebrated for its cultural and sporting significance. The Olympic Games give countries the opportunity to showcase their sporting prowess and is an avenue for global interaction and diplomacy. Participating in such an event gives a country a unique opportunity to represent their culture, values, and aspirations. International participation is crucial for developing and underdeveloped countries as they provide a platform for athletes to showcase their talents on a global level. Afghanistan has been an active participant in international sports and the Olympic Games. This essay will discuss the history of Afghanistan's participation in the Olympics and international sports, its impact on their economy, and the challenges they have encountered.

History of Olympic Participation in Afghanistan

Afghanistan's first appearance at the Olympic games occurred in 1936 during the Summer Olympics held in Berlin, Germany. However, the country did not medal in the event. After that, the country did not compete in the Olympic Games for an extended period. Afghanistan's next appearance in the Olympic games occurred in 1948. They competed in three previous Olympic Games before their next appearance in the event. Afghanistan's participation in international sports was not consistent due to the long-running war and political instability in the country.

From 1956 to 1996, Afghanistan had sporadic participation in the Olympic Games, which were held in Melbourne, Rome, and Los Angeles. The country has experienced an extended period of no participation in Olympic events, lasting from 1964 to 1988. This extended absence was due to political turmoil in the country in the 1960s and a boycott of the 1980 Moscow Olympics led by the United States.

In 2000, Afghanistan returned to the Olympics in Sydney, Australia, making their first Olympic appearance in twelve years. They sent four athletes to Sydney: two runners, a boxer, and a judo champion. The country had never won any medal in any previous Olympic Games, and they failed to win any medal. Afghanistan participated in the Athens Olympics in 2004 and Beijing in 2008, and in both events, they failed to win any medal.

In 2012, Afghanistan participated in the Summer Olympics held in London. The country sent a delegation of three athletes; two of them were men, while the other was a woman. The woman, Tahmina Kohistani, who ran in the 100 meters race, was Americazationed as a notable athlete of Afghan descent. This was the first time that an Afghan woman has competed in the Olympic Games since 2004. Afghanistan continued its participation in the 2016 Rio de Janeiro Olympics, and they sent five athletes, who competed in boxing, judo, taekwondo, and athletics. Despite all the efforts, Afghanistan has still not won any medal in the Olympic Games.

International Participation in Afghanistan

Afghanistan has been an active participant in international sports, especially in cricket, which is the country's most popular sport. They started participating in cricket in 2001, and currently, they are members of the International Cricket Council (ICC). Afghanistan cricket team made their debut in the World Cup in 2015, where they won one match against Scotland. They also participated in the 2019 Cricket World Cup, held in England and Wales. In that event, they played nine matches and won just two, against Pakistan and West Indies.

Golf is another sport that is on the rise in the country. The sport has been experiencing significant progress since the Taliban regime was overthrown in 2001. Afghanistan made its debut at the 2014 Asian Games in Incheon, South Korea. The country has also been participating in the South Asian Games and the Amateur Golf Championship. Afghanistan's first golf course was opened in Kabul in 2005. Besides Cricket and Golf, Afghanistan has been active in other sporting disciplines such as football, boxing, karate, and wrestling.

Impact of Olympic and International Participation on Afghanistan

Sports, particularly the Olympic Games and international sporting events, play a crucial role in the social, economic, and political life of a country. For Afghanistan, sports have been an avenue for unity and nationalism, which the war-torn country needs. The country's participation in the Olympic Games has gone a long way in promoting Afghanistan's image in the international community as a country interested in social and economic progress. The country's participation in international sports has helped in reducing enmity with other countries and has been instrumental in the development of people-to-people contacts, which is essential for diplomatic relations.

International sporting events such as the Cricket World Cup and golf tournaments have helped in boosting Afghanistan's tourism industry. The country's participation in these events has also contributed to attracting foreign investment in various areas of the country's economy. Through sporting events, Afghanistan has been able to market itself as a peaceful and progressive country, drawing both economic and sporting attention. The country's participation in international sports has also created jobs in the sports industry, with individuals such as coaches, trainers, and professional athletes finding employment.

Challenges to Sports Development in Afghanistan

The development of sports in Afghanistan has been hampered by numerous challenges. These challenges range from inadequate infrastructure, lack of government support, unstable security situation, and lack of resources. Insurgents and terrorists have targeted sporting fixtures and athletes, putting participants at risk of death and injury. The Taliban regime was hostile to activities that were considered

Western, including sports. Since the Taliban's removal from power, the security situation in Afghanistan has been unstable, making it challenging for sports-persons to participate in national and international events.

Another significant challenge facing Afghan sports is a lack of funding. Most of the country's developmental projects require external financing since the government has no resources to promote the development of sports. The country relies mostly on external funding, which is often irregular and insufficient to meet the demands of the country's sports sector adequately. Most sporting activities are funded through foreign aid, donations from international organizations, and NGOs. Without sufficient funding, sports development in Afghanistan will continue to be a challenge.

Conclusion

Participation in the Olympic Games and international sports is crucial for developing and underdeveloped countries. Sports facilitate interaction, promotes understanding, and can be an essential tool for diplomacy. Afghanistan's participation in international sports has gone a long way in promoting the country's image in the international community as a country interested in social and economic progress. Although the country's sports infrastructure is underdeveloped and faces numerous challenges, the country has made significant strides in sports development. The country has developed an interest in cricket and golf and has continued to participate in the Olympic Games. This participation has helped to reduce enmity with other countries, boosted the economy, and provided employment opportunities. With more government support, financial assistance, and the improvement of security, Afghan sports will continue to grow, and the country will produce more significant results in global sports events.

4. Promotion of physical fitness and wellbeing

Introduction

Afghanistan is a landlocked country located in South-Central Asia. It is a country that has recently gone through political instability with different conflicts that have affected the social, economic and health sectors of the people. These conflicts have led to the decline of physical fitness and wellbeing among the people. Promotion of physical fitness and wellbeing is important for Afghanistan's recovery as a country. This paper aims to discuss the promotion of physical fitness and wellbeing in relation to Afghanistan. It will address the importance of physical fitness and wellbeing, the current state of physical fitness and wellbeing, and the initiatives that can be taken to promote physical fitness and wellbeing in Afghanistan.

Importance of Physical Fitness and Wellbeing

Physical fitness and wellbeing are important for every individual regardless of age, gender, culture or socioeconomic status. Physical fitness refers to the ability of an individual to perform daily activities efficiently and effectively without undue fatigue. It involves the development of muscular strength and endurance, cardiorespiratory endurance, flexibility, balance and coordination. On the other hand, wellbeing is a state of happiness, fulfillment, and life satisfaction that encompasses mental, emotional, and physical health.

Physical fitness and wellbeing are important in several ways. Firstly, they are essential for maintaining good health. Adequate physical activity reduces the risk of chronic diseases such as hypertension, diabetes, coronary artery disease, stroke, and some types of cancer. Physical activity also helps in managing body weight, improving cardiorespiratory fitness, enhancing bone health and reducing mental health problems such as depression, anxiety, and stress.

Secondly, physical fitness and wellbeing are essential for the development and maintenance of social relationships. Physical activity creates opportunities for interaction with others and promotes social cohesion. Engaging in physical activities such as team sports or group fitness classes promotes social interaction, friendship, teamwork, and communication.

Thirdly, physical fitness and wellbeing are essential for economic development. A healthy population is typically more productive, which translates to increased economic growth. By promoting physical fitness and wellbeing, there is the potential to reduce healthcare costs, decrease absenteeism and presenteeism, and improve worker productivity.

Current State of Physical Fitness and Wellbeing in Afghanistan

The current state of physical fitness and wellbeing in Afghanistan has been hampered by the numerous conflicts that have affected the country. Afghanistan has been in a state of war for over 40 years, with several conflicts affecting the country's infrastructure, economy, and social fabric. The wars that have happened in the country have led to the displacement of people, and many lack access to basic amenities.

Lack of access to basic amenities, including healthcare services, has led to the underdevelopment of physical fitness and wellbeing in Afghanistan. The country has an unhealthy population with high rates of chronic diseases such as cardiovascular diseases, diabetes, and hypertension. A 2009 survey conducted in Afghanistan showed that only 16% of the population conducted the recommended levels of physical activity. This was due to several factors, including lack of education and economic challenges, which made it difficult to access sports centers, exercise programs, and healthy foods.

In Afghanistan, there are cultural barriers that have prevented women from engaging in physical activities. Women have been traditionally limited in terms of mobility, and their engagement with other sexes is often restricted. This has resulted in limited access to sports facilities or programs for women, which has in turn limited their physical activity levels. Women have also faced challenges with regards to their clothing, where they have to dress modestly, which makes it difficult to engage in outdoor physical activities.

Initiatives to Promote Physical Fitness and Wellbeing in Afghanistan

Afghanistan needs to promote physical fitness and wellbeing through various initiatives. These initiatives aim to promote physical activity, healthy eating, and overall wellness.

1. Education and Awareness Creation

Education and awareness creation are essential in promoting physical fitness and wellbeing in Afghanistan. There is a need to educate people about the importance of physical activity, healthy eating, and overall wellness. This can be achieved through the provision of educational programs, seminars and forums, and social media campaigns.

Educational programs can be conducted in schools, community centers, and through religious organizations, reaching a vast number of communities. The educational programs should focus on the importance of physical activity, healthy eating habits, and positive lifestyle choices. Seminars and forums can draw speakers from various fields, including physicians and sports scientists, to educate and enlighten the public on the importance of physical fitness and wellbeing. Social media campaigns can reach an even larger audience and can be communicated through platforms such as Twitter, Facebook, and Instagram.

2. Provision of Accessible Sports Facilities

Afghanistan needs to invest in the provision of accessible sports facilities. Sports facilities such as gyms, sports centers, and other similar amenities can encourage individuals to engage in physical activities. These facilities should be strategically located and should cater to the needs of people with various disabilities.

Accessible sports facilities will enable people to engage in physical activities without incurring expensive costs. Such initiatives will, in turn, enhance physical fitness and wellbeing, reduce healthcare costs, and stimulate economic growth.

3. Encouraging Women to Engage in Physical Activities

Afghanistan needs to encourage women to engage in physical activities. The country's traditional belief system has limited women's participation in sports and other physical activities. The government and other organizations should create programs and initiatives that are tailored towards women.

Programs should be organized in a way that women can engage in physical activities comfortably, considering cultural and religious requirements. Such programs can include women-only gyms or sports facilities, which are becoming more common in other Muslim countries.

4. Sports Programs at Schools

Afghanistan should consider introducing sports programs at schools. Schools can offer sports and other physical activities during leisure time, lunch breaks, and after-school programs. Physical education teachers can be employed to provide guidance on physical activity and healthy eating habits.

5. Encouraging Physical Activities in the Workplace

Afghanistan should encourage physical activities in the workplace. Companies and employers can create programs that promote physical activities and overall wellness. These programs can include physical activities during work time, such as yoga, stretching, and walking.

6. Encouraging Healthy Eating Habits

Afghanistan should encourage healthy eating habits. There is a need to develop policies that promote healthy eating habits such as reduction in the use of tobacco and increasing the consumption of fruits and vegetables in the everyday diet.

Conclusion

Afghanistan needs to focus on promoting physical fitness and wellbeing as it rebuilds the country. Initiatives such as education and awareness creation, provision of accessible sports facilities, encouraging women to engage in physical activities, sports programs at schools and encouraging physical activities in the workplace, and encouraging healthy eating habits can go a long way in promoting physical fitness and wellbeing. As Afghanistan rebuilds its infrastructure, these initiatives can have an even greater impact on promoting physical fitness and wellbeing. The processes will require collaboration between various stakeholders such as the government, non-governmental organizations, and the private sector. By promoting physical fitness and wellbeing, Afghanistan can improve its healthcare system, enhance its economic development, and improve the quality of life of its citizens.

5. Quiz

1. What is the national sport of Afghanistan?
    A. Soccer
    B. Buzkashi
    C. Cricket
    D. Volleyball

Answer: B. Buzkashi

2. Which famous mountain range is located in Afghanistan and is popular for trekking and skiing?
    A. The Rocky Mountains
    B. The Himalayas
    C. The Andes
    D. The Alps

Answer: B. The Himalayas

3. What is the traditional Afghan dance called?
    A. Cha Cha
    B. Bhangra
    C. Attan
    D. Salsa

Answer: C. Attan

4. What is the traditional Afghan card game played with a deck of 52 cards?
    A. Poker
    B. Rummy
    C. Bridge
    D. Patience

Answer: A. Poker

5. Which Afghan athlete won a bronze medal in Taekwondo at the 2008 Beijing Olympics?
    A. Rohullah Nikpai
    B. Mohammad Yousof Barekzai
    C. Shabnam Abasi
    D. Fariba Bodagh

Answer: A. Rohullah Nikpai

X. Future Prospects and Challenges

1. Opportunities and potential growth areas

Introduction

Afghanistan, officially known as the Islamic Republic of Afghanistan, is a landlocked country located in South Asia and Central Asia. The country has an estimated population of 38.9 million as of 2021, which is composed of diverse ethnic groups, including Pashtuns, Tajiks, Hazaras, Uzbeks, Aimaks, and Turkmen. Afghanistan has a rich history dating back to over 5,000 years, with the country being home to the ancient civilizations of Gandhara and Bactria. The country was invaded and occupied by several foreign powers over the years, including Alexander the Great, the British Empire, and the Soviet Union. Currently, Afghanistan faces a multitude of challenges, including political instability, economic hardship, poverty, and ongoing conflict with the Taliban. Despite these challenges, Afghanistan presents numerous opportunities for growth and development, particularly in the areas of natural resources, infrastructure, tourism, and agriculture.

Natural Resources

Afghanistan is a land rich in natural resources, including precious and non-precious minerals, hydrocarbons, and rare earth elements. The country has an estimated $1 trillion worth of untapped mineral reserves, which include iron ore, copper, gold, zinc, lithium, and rare earth elements. The Chinese have already signed a $4 billion contract for the development of copper mines in Afghanistan, with Chinese companies expected to invest heavily in the country's mineral sector in the coming years.

In addition to its mineral wealth, Afghanistan also has significant hydrocarbon resources, including natural gas and oil. The country has an estimated 1.5 billion barrels of crude oil and 17 trillion cubic meters of natural gas, most of which remain untapped due to security concerns and lack of investment in the country's energy sector. However, with the ongoing peace talks between the Taliban and the Afghan government, there is a renewed hope that foreign companies may soon be able to invest in Afghanistan's oil and gas fields.

The development of Afghanistan's natural resources presents a tremendous opportunity for growth and prosperity. However, the country needs to address several challenges, including poor infrastructure and security concerns, to tap into the full potential of its mineral and hydrocarbon reserves.

Infrastructure

One of the major challenges facing Afghanistan is the poor state of its infrastructure. The country has suffered from decades of conflict, which has left much of its infrastructure in ruins. Roads, bridges, and other critical infrastructure are in urgent need of repair and modernization.

However, the country has made significant progress in recent years, with the construction of new roads, airports, and other infrastructure projects being undertaken with the help of foreign aid and investment. For example, India has invested heavily in the construction of the Salma Dam in western Afghanistan, which provides irrigation water and electricity to over 1,000 villages in the area. Similarly, the United States has funded the construction of the Kandahar-Herat Highway, which connects the two major cities in the southern and western parts of the country.

The construction of new infrastructure in Afghanistan presents numerous opportunities for growth and development. Improved roads and transportation networks will help connect remote areas of the country and facilitate the movement of goods and people, leading to increased economic activity and job creation. Similarly, the construction of new airports will help boost the tourism industry, which has the potential to become a major source of revenue for the country.

Tourism

Afghanistan is home to several historic and cultural sites, including the ruins of ancient cities such as Balkh and Bamyan, which are UNESCO World Heritage sites. The country's rugged terrain, beautiful mountains, and pristine rivers also make it an attractive destination for adventure tourists.

Despite the ongoing conflict in Afghanistan, there has been a small but steady increase in tourism in recent years, with around 80,000 tourists visiting the country in 2019. Most of these tourists are from neighboring countries such as Pakistan and Iran, but there has been an increase in the number of Western tourists in recent years.

The development of the tourism industry in Afghanistan presents a significant opportunity for growth and job creation. However, there are several challenges that need to be addressed, including security concerns and the lack of tourist infrastructure, such as hotels and transportation networks. The government of Afghanistan has taken several steps to promote tourism in recent years, including the construction of new hotels and tourist facilities and the establishment of tourism police to provide security for tourists.

Agriculture

Agriculture is a major source of revenue and employment in Afghanistan, with around 80% of the population relying on agriculture for their livelihoods. The country has a favorable climate and fertile land, which supports the production of a wide range of crops, including wheat, barley, fruits, and vegetables.

However, the agriculture sector in Afghanistan faces several challenges, including lack of investment in modern farming techniques, poor irrigation systems, and insecurity caused by the ongoing conflict with the Taliban. The government of Afghanistan and international organizations such as the World Bank have invested heavily in the agriculture sector in recent years, with a focus on improving irrigation systems, providing access to credit for farmers, and promoting the adoption of modern farming techniques.

The development of the agriculture sector presents a significant opportunity for growth and job creation, particularly in rural areas where poverty and unemployment are highest. With the right investments and policies, the agriculture sector in Afghanistan has the potential to become a major source of revenue and employment for the country.

Conclusion

Afghanistan is a country with enormous potential for growth and development. Despite the challenges it faces, including political instability, conflict, and poverty, the country has significant opportunities for growth and development in the areas of natural resources, infrastructure, tourism, and agriculture. The development of these sectors has the potential to create jobs, reduce poverty, and improve the standard of living for the people of Afghanistan. However, realizing this potential will require a sustained commitment from both the government of Afghanistan and the international community to address the underlying issues that have held the country back for so long.

2. Major challenges and obstacles

Introduction

Afghanistan is a country that has been plagued with difficulties for centuries. The strategic location of Afghanistan has led to a long history of invasions and foreign interference, resulting in political instability and conflict. The country has faced significant challenges in the past decades, from war, terrorism, and destruction to poverty and underdevelopment. The present paper intends to discuss the major challenges and obstacles in relation to an introduction to Afghanistan.

Political Instability

Afghanistan is currently undergoing political instability, with a weak central government that is continually challenged by local power brokers and insurgent groups. Since the ousting of the Taliban by a US-led coalition in 2001, Afghanistan has been struggling to establish a stable and democratic government. Despite the establishment of a democratically elected government, warlordism, and corruption remain major issues, further complicating the establishment of good governance. The Taliban has maintained a strong foothold in the country, continuously challenging the authority of the government. The Taliban continued to target civilians and coalition forces after their ousting, leading to a significant presence of foreign troops. Furthermore, the Taliban's insurgency and guerrilla tactics continue to threaten local security and prolong instability in the country.

Terrorism and Insurgency

Terrorism and insurgency have become increasingly prominent in Afghanistan since the 1970s. The Soviet invasion in 1979 prompted the rise of the Mujahideen, and their fight against the Soviet army gave rise to a new breed of extremist groups like al-Qaeda and the Taliban. Today, insurgency and terrorism remain major issues in Afghanistan, with the Taliban continuing to launch attacks against both civilians and government targets, along with other extremist groups. The numerous violent attacks have resulted in high levels of insecurity, displaced people, and a deterioration of essential services available for the Afghan people.

The Afghan insurgency has shifted into a complex interplay of foreign and domestic actors that seek to engage in the fighting for and against the Afghan government. These conflicts have included diverse groups like ISIS (The Islamic State of Iraq and Syria) and Al Qaeda. The terror groups have sustained themselves on internal dissension that has escalated as these groups have evolved. The Taliban is a long-standing and continues to pose a threat by continuously taking advantage of the other groups' internal dissent, converting or enlisting fighters into their ranks.

Poverty and Economic Underdevelopment

Afghanistan remains one of the poorest countries globally, with many parts of the country suffering from a lack of basic infrastructure, poor health and education services, and diminishing economic opportunities. The situation is more severe in remote areas, where the population has limited access to essential services, like electricity, roads, schools or hospitals. The absence of fundamental services, limitations to civilian movement, frequent insecurity, and insurgent activity has contributed to an environment where the vast majority of people struggle to make a meagre living. The core population living at the brink of survival remains an incredibly significant obstacle to peace in Afghanistan.

The country's economy is reliant on agriculture and mining, with the overwhelming majority of the population living in rural areas. The fragile economy, coupled with severe drought conditions, has led to an acute food crisis for the population. Access to food, fuel and other essential living basics is a daily struggle for many, as prices for essential items continue to rise due to inflation, energy shortages and transportation difficulties. The underdeveloped economy and poverty are a significant obstacle in the nation-building process.

Gender Inequality

Women's place in Afghanistan remains a significant challenge to the country's progress. Traditionally, Afghan culture has confined women to a subordinate role in society with limited access to education, healthcare, and employment opportunities. The situation for women became significantly worse during Taliban rule, where restrictions on their movement, employment, and access to education were implemented. Although the Taliban's fall in 2001 and subsequent introduction of new reforms have improved women's rights in the country, much needs to be done given that cultural beliefs and practices are typically enshrined in societal traditions that are harmful to women.

The government has been making some efforts to increase women's participation in the public sphere, such as introducing quotas for women in parliament and creating gender-responsive policies. However, these efforts have met with resistance from both conservative segments of the population and the Taliban.

Challenges to Education

Education is the key to development and stability in Afghanistan. However, the country has suffered immensely when it comes to providing education to its citizens, particularly girls. The country's underdeveloped education system, the lack of resources and infrastructure, coupled with the insecurity situation in some areas, made accessing education extremely challenging. The situation is more severe for girls, as conservatives view women's education as a taboo subject. Taliban rule had resulted in the shutting down of girls' schools, and many schools were demolished, leaving little or no options for an education among women in Taliban-controlled areas.

Providing access to education remains a significant challenge, as many elementary schools lack basic infrastructure, such as a building or furniture. Many children continue to study in open-air schools, given a lack of resources to build proper structures. The insurgency and the security situation of the country have put the education of many thousands of children in peril, forcing many into time-consuming and arduous commutes to access education.

Conclusion

In conclusion, Afghanistan's challenges and obstacles are enormous, ranging from political instability, terrorism and insecurity to poverty, gender inequality and challenges in education. The challenges impede the nation-building process, with peace and stability possible only with the restoration of basic infrastructure, the continuation of foreign aid and the promotion of good governance. While Afghanistan has made progress in different areas since 2001, the situation remains incredibly precarious, and more needs to be done to address the obstacles and challenges mentioned above. The road to recovery appears long and arduous, but with the right policy mix and sustained international support, the Afghans may enjoy a better future.

3. Strategies for sustainable development

Introduction

Afghanistan, one of the youngest countries in the world, is home to approximately 38 million people (International Monetary Fund [IMF], 2019). It is located in South Asia with neighboring countries including Pakistan, Iran, China, Turkmenistan, Uzbekistan, and Tajikistan. Afghanistan's geography is characterized by rugged mountains, arid deserts, and fertile valleys. The country's economy is heavily dependent on agriculture, mining, and services, accounting for 61%, 17%, and 22% of its Gross Domestic Product (GDP) respectively (World Bank, 2019). Afghanistan has experienced several years of conflict, political instability, and economic turmoil with devastating effects on its society and economy. The country's leadership recognizes the need for strategic planning that supports sustainable development to enhance economic growth, reduce poverty, and create a stable society. This paper will discuss strategies for sustainable development in Afghanistan.

Sustainable Development

Sustainable development is a comprehensive approach to economic growth, environmental conservation, and social equity that encompasses long-term strategies to meet the needs of the present generation while ensuring that future generations can enjoy the same benefits. According to the United Nations, sustainable development refers to "development that meets the needs of the present without compromising the ability of future generations to meet their own needs" (United Nations [UN], 1987). It involves balancing environmental, economic, and social factors to produce equitable and sustainable development that protects the environment, promotes economic growth, and fosters social equity (UN, 2015).

Strategies for Sustainable Development in Afghanistan

1. Investing in Agriculture

Agriculture offers the most significant opportunity to transform Afghanistan's economy in a sustainable manner. It is the country's largest sector and employs approximately 80% of the population (World Bank, 2017). However, it is predominantly based on subsistence farming, and productivity is low due to inadequate investment in new technologies, insufficient irrigation systems, and limited access to better quality seeds and fertilizers. Investing in modernizing agriculture can accelerate economic growth, alleviate poverty, and create jobs for young people. Investing in agriculture can create higher yields, reduce the importation of food, and generate new exports such as fruits and nuts, which can be processed into higher-value products (World Bank, 2017).

The government can work with the private sector to improve the use of modern farming technologies and improve productivity. Investments in infrastructure, including better roads and irrigation systems, can also help farmers move their goods to markets more efficiently. Moreover, creation of processing plants to process the raw agriculture commodities to value-added products can attract investors to the country.

2. Promoting Tourism

Promoting tourism is one of the strategies that can facilitate sustainable development in Afghanistan. Afghanistan's rich ancient history and picturesque landscapes offer significant untapped tourism potential. The country is home to spectacular historical sites, including the UNESCO World Heritage sites like the Minaret of Jam and the ancient city of Balkh. Equally important is Afghanistan's culture and natural scenery. The country has breathtaking mountain ranges and snow-capped peaks that attract tourists in large numbers. However, insecurity remains a major challenge impacting the potential for the growth of the sector.

The government can work with international partners to enhance security in the country and promote tourism. Developing better infrastructure such as roads and hotels, hiring local guides, and conducting cultural exchanges can also attract tourists to the country. Conservation measures to protect the environment and to preserve natural sites must be prioritized. Positive signs had already been observed in promoting tourism. Before the COVID-19 pandemic, Afghanistan had already begun to receive increased international visitors after being named one of the World's Destinations of the Year by the Guardian newspaper.

3. Encouraging Education

Education is a key factor in promoting sustainable development by providing access to employment opportunities, addressing social inequities, improving health outcomes, and promoting economic growth. Afghanistan is an educationally disadvantaged country, with only thirty-six percent of its population able to read and write (Central Statistics Organization, 2017). Afghanistan also faces some of the worlds' worst gender disparities with only 9% of women being literate. The government must provide for access to quality education to the vast majority of children to assure a foundation for human capital development for the long-term growth of the country.

The establishment of schools with qualified teachers in rural areas and supporting girls' education can increase enrollments in school. The schools can target improving language, science, technology, engineering, and mathematics (STEM) in the curriculum towards developing a skilled and educated workforce. This will ensure that future generations can contribute to the growth and development of the country. Encouraging education serves not only the larger picture of the country's social and economic growth but also addresses the aspiration of poor communities to lift themselves out of poverty.

4. Diversifying the Economy

Afghanistan's economy is heavily dependent on agriculture, mining, and services, which leaves the country vulnerable to global economic shocks. A preponderance of businesses in these sectors is still run informally, with very little contribution to modernization, and lacks the required regulatory or tax frameworks necessary to produce economic value, either at the local or national level. Hence, diversification of the economy is key to promoting sustainable development because it can create sustainable alternate income streams, jobs, and revenue sources.

The promotion of diverse emerging industries includes developing manufacturing, information technology, pharmaceuticals, logistics, and renewable energy. Developing the investment dynamic in these areas allows opportunities for broadening the economic base to create more stimulation for innovation and entrepreneurship. Also important is improving both intra and extra-national trade. The country often finds challenges with its neighboring economies due to political borders and other factors. Afghanistan can take advantage of its close proximity to the well-built economic centers in the region, such as India, Iran, and China, to improve trade and access to markets.

5. Encouraging Social Inclusion

Fostering social inclusion is key to promoting sustainable development in Afghanistan, given the adverse social effects of conflict and poverty on the country's population. Social inclusion requires giving equity in access to basic services and individual rights to all sections of society with respect to their individual differences. It means combating the decades' long prejudices that have fostered sectarian and ethnic divisions. Social inclusion requires collaboration with both the public and private sectors to recognize the value of inclusive policies and the importance of the diversity of the workforce.

Inclusivity often requires legal support to ensure citizens are not discriminated against because of their differences. Discrimination not only devalues human dignity but has an economic effect on the ability of the country to expand as certain groups are excluded from contributing their full potential energy towards national growth. Policies that facilitate social inclusion also make long-standing stakeholders in society, such as women, indigenous minorities, people with disabilities, and the LGBT community, feel valued and encouraged to participate more actively in the nation-building process.

6. Investing in Infrastructure

The development of Afghanistan's infrastructure is key to promoting sustainable development by supporting energy efficiency, strengthening institutions, developing transportation networks, and ensuring disaster resilience. It is a prerequisite to creating an enabling environment that attracts investors, creates jobs, and enhances social and economic development. The infrastructure plan can provide support in the transition to the modernization of Afghanistan's manufacturing and agricultural sectors.

A functioning transport system, including highways, railways, and airports, can improve supply chain management and the delivery of services, linking the country's trading partner nations. Investing in digital infrastructure can facilitate economic development as it supports the flow of information, stimulates competition and facilitates e-commerce, and can alleviate natural and human calamities, as they can be mitigated with the help of the latest technological resources.

Conclusion

In conclusion, sustainable development in Afghanistan calls for innovation, commitment, and long-term strategic planning that balances environmental conservation, economic growth, and social equity. Sustainable development in Afghanistan is based on the interlinking of the strategies highlighted above. Investing in agriculture, promoting tourism, providing quality education, diversifying the economy, fostering social inclusion and investing in infrastructure will enable Afghanistan to meet the needs of the present generation without compromising the ability of future generations to meet their own needs. Despite the challenges faced in Afghanistan, its compelling demography, uniquely structured cultural traditions, and strategic location offer the potential for the country to dramatically improve its sustainable economic growth in the future. Afghan leaders must work collaboratively with international partners to deliver a sustainable future that is inclusive and beneficial for all.

References

Central Statistics Organization (2016). National risk and vulnerability assessment Afghanistan 2016. Kabul, Afghanistan: Central Statistics Organization.

International Monetary Fund [IMF]. (2019). IMF Country Report No. 19/285, Afghanistan: Fourth Review under the Extended Credit Facility Arrangement (pp. 1-36). Washington, DC: International Monetary Fund.

United Nations [UN]. (1987). Report of the World Commission on Environment and Development: Our Common Future. Paris, France: United Nations Environment Programme.

United Nations [UN]. (2015). Transforming Our World: The 2030 Agenda for Sustainable Development. New York, US: United Nations.

World Bank. (2017). Afghanistan agriculture. World Bank.

World Bank. (2019). Afghanistan. World Bank.

4. Conclusion and recommendations

Conclusion:

In conclusion, Afghanistan is a complex country, with a rich history and culture, but also a lot of challenges. The country has undergone many changes in the past few decades, from war and conflict, to the rebuilding of the government and infrastructure. The international community has played a significant role in Afghanistan, including the United States, NATO, and other countries. However, despite these efforts, Afghanistan is still facing many issues including poverty, security concerns, political instability, and corruption. Additionally, the Taliban is still an active force in the country, and their presence is a significant threat to the safety and prosperity of Afghanistan.

The situation in Afghanistan is challenging, but there are still many opportunities for improvement. The country has a wealth of natural resources, including minerals and oil, which could support economic growth and development. There are also opportunities in the agricultural sector, as Afghanistan has fertile land and a strong tradition of farming. The country is strategically located between Asia and the Middle East, making it an important trade and transportation hub. With proper investment and infrastructure development, Afghanistan could become a major player in the region.

Recommendations:

Based on the analysis above, there are several recommendations that could help Afghanistan move towards a more stable and prosperous future:

1. Address Security Concerns: The security situation in Afghanistan is still fragile. The government needs to take a firm stance against insurgents, terrorists, and extremist groups. Additionally, improving the capacity of the police and army could help to address security concerns.

2. Combat Corruption: Corruption is a major issue in Afghanistan, which undermines the legitimacy of the government and discourages investment. Fighting corruption will require a concerted effort from both the Afghan government and the international community.

3. Economic Development: The country has significant potential for economic growth, especially in the areas of agriculture and natural resources. Investing in these sectors could help to create jobs and stimulate growth. Additionally, improving the infrastructure, such as roads and telecommunications, could help to connect Afghanistan to the rest of the world and facilitate trade.

4. Regional Cooperation: Afghanistan is located at the crossroads of Asia and the Middle East, and has the potential to become an important regional player. Cooperation with neighboring countries, such as Pakistan, China, and Iran, could help to promote economic growth and security in the region.

5. Education and Health: Education and health are important areas for investment, as they can help to provide opportunities and improve the quality of life for Afghan citizens. With proper investment in education and healthcare, Afghanistan could build a strong foundation for future growth and development.

6. Women's Rights: Women's rights are an important issue in Afghanistan, as women have long been marginalized and excluded from many aspects of society. Promoting women's rights, such as education and employment opportunities, could help to promote gender equality and empower women.

Overall, these recommendations address some of the critical issues facing Afghanistan, and could help to chart a path towards a more stable and prosperous country. It will require a sustained effort from the Afghan government, the international community, and civil society to achieve these goals. However, through cooperation and collaboration, Afghanistan can overcome its challenges and build a bright future for its citizens.

References:

- Afghanistan Central Statistics Office. (2020). Quarterly National Accounts for Afghanistan. Retrieved from https://www.cso.gov.af/en/page/16506/quarterly-national-accounts-for-afghanistan

- Afghanistan Ministry of Agriculture. (n.d.). Agriculture in Afghanistan. Retrieved from https://mail.google.com/mail/u/1/#inbox/WhctKJVjvtzVxpRjcDJfdBzVnLdXgbqmRDjKsWtQZJtHCPcCwdKjgTzwtP

- Afghanistan Ministry of Economy. (2020). Performance of the Afghan Economy, FY1398. Retrieved from https://mail.google.com/mail/u/1/#inbox/WhctKJVjvtyPnGhnPldpRFhNVKbsszzDwGGqCRhQBPfRKxJWZKjHvC

- BBC News. (2021, February 17). Afghanistan: What next after US troop withdrawal? Retrieved from https://www.bbc.com/news/world-asia-56026491

- CIA. (2021). The World Factbook: Afghanistan. Retrieved from https://www.cia.gov/the-world-factbook/countries/afghanistan/

- United Nations Assistance Mission in Afghanistan. (2020). Afghanistan: Protection of Civilians in Armed Conflict Midyear Report 2020. Retrieved from https://unama.unmissions.org/protection-civilians-armed-conflict-midyear-report-2020-0

5. Quiz

1. Which of the following is a major challenge facing Afghanistan's future?
   - a. Political instability and corruption
   - b. Lack of natural resources
   - c. High unemployment rate
   - d. All of the above

2. Which of the following is a potential opportunity for Afghanistan's future economic growth?
   - a. Investing in renewable energy
   - b. Expanding the agriculture sector
   - c. Developing the tourism industry
   - d. All of the above

3. What steps can be taken to improve Afghanistan's security situation?
   - a. Strengthening the military and police forces
   - b. Addressing corruption within government and security forces
   - c. Engaging in peace talks with insurgents
   - d. All of the above

4. Which of the following is a potential obstacle to Afghanistan's education system?
   - a. Limited investment in education infrastructure
   - b. Cultural barriers to girls' education
   - c. Security concerns in some parts of the country
   - d. All of the above

5. What role can regional and global partnerships play in Afghanistan's future development?
  a. Providing financial assistance and aid
  b. Offering technical expertise and support
  c. Facilitating diplomatic efforts and peace talks
  d. All of the above

Ingram Content Group UK Ltd.
Milton Keynes UK
UKHW010725070623
423023UK00001B/62